Master Your Life
Transformational "Quotes" Complete Workbook Series
~ 3 books in 1 ~
CONDENSED VERSION

Lucas J. Robak

www.LucasRobak.com
Lucas@LucasRobak.com
(414) 520-5163

Copyright © 2016 Authored by Lucas J. Robak
Published by Authorpreneur Academy
All rights reserved.

No part of this publication may be reproduced, stored in a retrieval system, or transmitted in any form or by any means, electronic, mechanical, photocopying, recording, scanning, or otherwise, except as permitted under Sections 107 or 108 of the 1976 US Copyright Act, without prior written permission of the publisher.

This publication is designed to provide information regarding the subject matter covered. However, it is sold with the understanding that the author and publisher are not engaged in rendering legal, financial, or other professional advice. Law and practices often vary from state to state, and if legal or other expert assistance is required, the services of a professional should be sought. The author and publisher specifically disclaim any liability that is incurred from the use or application of the contents of this book. Think for yourself and chose your own actions!

ISBN-13: 978-0-9904403-2-1
ISBN-10: 0-9904403-2-X
LCCN: 2014918597

INTRODUCTION

This is a very condensed version of the first three books in the *Master Your Life: Transformational Quotes Workbook Series*.

With 306 quotes laid out in the following pages, be sure to take time and reflect on each question as to how it pertains to your life.

The original workbook series is separated into systematic chapters. Before each chapter you're provided with why those types of quotes are important and helps you to think differently before even proceeding. That content is not published within this book.

The main purpose of developing the book like this is for those who travel, like using paperback books, and want to carry the whole set with them at once.

Take your time with this and really meditate on the questions!

Be Different, Be You!

Book 1 - page 1

Book 2 - page 45

Book 3 - page 86

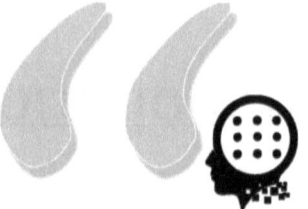

BOOK ONE

> What lies behind us and what lies before us are tiny matters compared to what lies within us.
> *- Ralph Waldo Emerson -*

The only things that matter are our thoughts. Nothing else! What you think determines who you are, who you will become, and how you will react. What happened to you is history; you already went through those situations. Your thoughts determine what you learned from those past incidents. What lies within us, our thoughts, determines our future. You can predict the future with your self-talk. You may not know how it will happen; all you need to know is that it will happen. You choose your own destiny. What you think determines your actions. Pay attention to your thinking. Choose your thoughts with care, and you will stand above the rest!

> Who is the person I want to become?
> When I catch myself thinking about senseless matters, what would I rather focus on? (Be specific.)
> What future do I want for myself?
> What thoughts can I think now which will bring this future to me?

> Choose a job you love, and you will never have to work a day in your life.
> *- Anonymous -*

When you do what you love, it does not feel like work. Many people believe they have no choice in their work, and that the work is merely a means to an end: to put a roof over their heads, food on the table, and survive. Viewed this way, there is no passion or joy in work when it is only about a paycheck. Other people give up six-figure incomes to make much less because they know there is more to life than money. If you do not love what you are doing, then why do it? Do not sell yourself out for a paycheck. When you do something you love, you will put more passion into it, get more creative, and care about all the aspects of it. When you do what you love, you will never look at it as work.

> How do the people in my life who love their jobs make me feel?
> How about the ones who hate their jobs?
> What are the five things I love doing most?
> What career fields can I pursue so I can do what I love every day?

> The more I want to get something done, the less I call it work.
> *- Richard Bach -*

Many people have negative perceptions about the idea of work: work is hard, boring, meaningless, dull, a pain, something to endure. Work hurts, tires you out, and drains your energy. Such negative beliefs lead you to hate working. A hateful state of mind is closed. Hate blocks creativity and disables positive passion. Let go of negative associations around work. None of that is true. Work makes the world go round. The truth is, all life is designed to do some kind of work. On the personal human level, work is a virtuous activity which keeps us from making mistakes, provides intrinsic self-worth, and is good for society. Work provides a sense of pride and confidence, helps others, supports families, builds community, reduces stress, helps us sleep better, and enables us to be responsible. Releasing negative ideas opens the door to discovering your passion. You'll know you have found your passion when time flies by. You will want to "work" 80 hours a week just so you don't have to work 40.

The point is, when you love what you're doing, you reap the deep rewards of work. You are always free to choose your thoughts, beliefs, actions. Free to make new choices. Free to live your passion. Many create miserable, hate-filled lives by clinging to limiting beliefs, believing they are prisoners with no choice but to endure pain, boredom, and misery to put food on the table and to buy useless material items which make them only temporarily happy. To get things done and live a life of joy, let go of negative ideas, and choose what you love to do every day.

What do I love doing for hours on end?
How will my community benefit from me pursuing that?
How can I make money doing that?

Do not go where the path may lead, go instead where there is no path and leave a trail.
- Ralph Waldo Emerson -

When you take a path which has already been set, it is safe. You will end up where everyone else ends up. You no longer give yourself a choice to develop your own voice and be who you are. A path is there to take you to a predetermined destination which you do not choose; it is where everyone else goes. Yes, making your own path is harder, but you have the power to end up where you want to be. You choose which direction you want to go! Once you create a new path, others will use it too. Be a leader, be your own person, and create as many new paths as you can. Do not accept society saying that this is how you are supposed to do things. You can make decisions on your own and go where you want. Stop letting other people and society control the direction you take in your life. Once you do something different, like living your passion, people will follow in your footsteps.

What results did I produce after creating my own path?
What was my satisfaction level after doing my own thing and creating my own path?
How can I create my own path in the near future?

Whenever you find yourself on the side of the majority, it is time to pause and reflect.
- Mark Twain -

Individuals may be extremely smart. When huge groups of people gather, they move in masses. Masses often end up following individuals who are great at taking initiative. It is natural for people to follow a leader who takes the initiative. However, that leader may be the most incompetent individual to walk this earth. Then the masses are following in the steps of incompetency. Wise people who see the movements of masses question the intelligence of leaders. What groups are you in? Start questioning the leaders in your life; look at their lives and determine if they are worth listening to and following. Never allow the masses to steal your passions!

> In what aspects of my life am I following the majority?
> What makes me different than everyone else?
> What success traits would I like to develop to become who I want to be?

Two roads diverged in a wood, and I—I took the one less traveled by, and that has made all the difference.
- Robert Frost -

As you walk through the woods and see two paths, the one less traveled will have more weeds, bushes, trees, and branches blocking the path. The road less traveled is harder to walk on because there are more obstacles, and it has the potential to be more risky. Each path leads to two different destinations: the path that is clean and unobstructed will lead you to the average person, with average results. The path which is obstructed will lead you to an extra-ordinarily successful life. Stop following the path beaten down by the crowd. Be your own person and follow the road you are most passionate about, the overgrown one with obstacles. Take the road less traveled, take your road!

> What happened when I took the road less traveled?
> What difference did I make by not following the majority?
> What difference can I make in the future by taking the road less traveled?

The only person you are destined to become is the person you decide to be.
- Ralph Waldo Emerson -

If you do not believe in destiny, think again. Your destiny is what you choose it to be. The path you are currently on is taking you to the life you are destined to have, but you can change it in an instant. If you look back on your life and the choices you made, you were destined to be right where you are now. If you do not like where you are in life and do not change, you are destined to live your current situation forever. You can choose to be anything you want to be. Every day, you are presented with millions of choices. The decisions you make will create your destiny. Make decisions based on who you want to become, not on who others think you should become!

> For what qualities am I destined?
> What characteristics do I want to acquire?
> What do I want to be known for?

Try not to become a man of success, but rather, try to become a man of value.
~ Albert Einstein ~

Your definition of success is unique. Some define success by their bank account. Others define it by their impact on the lives around them. By focusing on becoming a valuable person, by giving and sharing your unique strengths, skills, and gifts, success flows back to you as a byproduct of your own value. Do not always think of how you can benefit from situations; think instead of how you can be of benefit to others. Success comes from helping people, both directly from being appreciated, and indirectly, by putting out into the world what will come back to you. When you are beneficial to others, they will see value in you. Right now, you are important! Prove that to yourself by acting the part. The best way to be successful is to help others become successful. The best way to be a leader is to develop leaders. Stop putting yourself first in all your situations, and be helpful. The value you put out will return to you in abundance.

How do the successful people in my life exhibit value to to others?
How are the people I know invaluable to me?
How can I be more helpful to others?

In my experience, there is only one motivation, and that is desire. No reasons or principle contain it or stand against it.
~ Jane Smiley ~

If you want something badly enough, you will do what you need to do in order for it to happen. Desire causes excuses to disappear. By having a desire for something, nothing will be able to stop you, except yourself. Obstacles become learning experiences, opportunities, and ways to make you grow. Desire will keep motivating you every day. When you fulfill your purpose, the desire to keep moving forward will bring endless energy to complete all the tasks you need to do. You will be doing things you have never imagined before; your desire will be that strong!

What am I currently motivated to do?
What do I desire to achieve?
What stopped me in the past which I will not allow to stop me again?
How will I successfully move past it?

The whole secret of a successful life is to find out what is one's destiny to do, and then do it.
~ Henry Ford ~

We are all destined to do something. If we all followed our destiny, this would be a perfect world. As babies, we know what we want, and will do anything to get it. It is our parents, teachers, friends, and neighbors that break us down and make us conform to society. We all once had innocent minds with dreams of possibility. As we grow up, we are told, "You cannot do this", "that is impossible," "you are not qualified," "you are too stupid," "why would you waste your time with that?","it will be very hard to do,", etc. After years of dream-stealing negativity, we become like everyone else, doing what we are told and what is expected of us. We are all better than that! Find your passion, find your purpose, seek out mentors, and invest in your personal development with books, courses, seminars, and classes. To live your destiny, follow your gut instincts, and do what you know is right every step of the way!

What was I born to do?
How will I benefit from my results after becoming successful?
How will others benefit after I become successful?

The only thing worse than being blind is having sight but no vision.
- Helen Keller -

Imagine being deaf and blind; that was Helen Keller's life. Blindness and deafness can stop people from living their dreams. But Keller showed the world another way. She chose not to accept these as limiting factors; she saw them as assets. Those who see challenges as assets have vision. When you do not have a voice, you allow life to push you around because you have no ambition to pursue the dreams which you do not have. The greatest people in the world have purpose and vision; they are able to imagine and see the end result as successful. By keeping the successful end in sight, you keep motivated, and that will help you unfold the next step in the process of making your dream reality. Believe your dream is possible, and do not let anyone take that away from you!

What limiting factors of mine can be viewed as assets?
What is one vision of mine I want to see as a reality? Why?
What does my end result look, feel, and sound like?

First, have a definite, clear practical ideal; a goal, an objective. Second, have the necessary means to achieve your ends; wisdom, money, materials, and methods. Third, adjust all your means to that end.
- Aristotle -

Start with the end in mind. Figure out what it is you want to become in life. Set goals and have objectives to reach them. Once you know where you want to go, determine what knowledge you should acquire, how much money you will need, the materials you will use, and the different methods you can implement. Once you have all this information, make adjustments in your life to acquire all the means it will take to accomplish your objective. If you do not have the knowledge, start reading, go to trainings, seminars, workshops, and ask experts. If you do not have the money, borrow it, get loans, or use crowdfunding sites like kickstarter.com or gofundme.com. Where there is a will, there is always a way. Figure out the way, and stop at nothing to obtain your desires.

What is my one, clear, practical objective?
What knowledge do I still need to acquire?

Where will I find it?
What options do I have for the different methods I can implement?

Definiteness of purpose is the starting point of all achievement.
~ W. Clement Stone ~

When you travel, you need to know where you are starting and where you are going in order to know when you get there. Knowing your definite purpose in life will help you decide what goals to set and how to react to situations that arise along the way. Your personal purpose statement is a guide for all the decisions you will face along the way. Your purpose is vital to your success in every area of life. Those who are successful have a definite purpose, whether they consciously know it or not. By knowing why you exist, your decisions, goals, and where to begin will become easy! By discovering your life purpose, you will know what you need to do each day to fulfill it. Knowing why you exist, you will know what to do and how to do it. This is your guide for all your decisions.

What do I believe I was put on this earth to do?
How will discovering my life purpose benefit the world around me?
What is my life purpose? (HINT: Sum up all previous answers in 35 words or less)

You become what you believe.
~ Oprah Winfrey ~

"Your personal perception of reality is determined by the beliefs you hold," said psychiatrist and personal change expert, Abigail Brenner, M.D., referencing many confirming published studies. Further, you become what you believe. Beliefs are set in us during early childhood by parents, teachers, peers, and neighbors. People can go their entire lives believing or not believing in themselves because of what they learned before the age of 17. If you are a parent, teacher, or any adult figure in a child's life, leave other people's dreams alone. If you are an adult who had a negative self-belief instilled by adults in your life growing up, remember: you have a choice in what you agree with. Just because they believe you are not capable of greatness does not mean you need to believe that as well. Everyone can change, but first, one needs to believe in change. Believe in yourself. You have the power to change your life into whatever it is you want to create. Believe you can, and you will! There is no one stopping you but yourself. If someone tells you that your beliefs and ideas are stupid or impossible, there is no need to ever listen to them again because they are small thinkers. Be a big thinker!

What do I want to believe I can do?
What is the perception I want for myself?
How can I practice believing in myself?

Whether you think you can or think you can't, you're right.
~ Henry Ford ~

When you think something is impossible, you immediately start coming up with all the reasons why it is impossible. When you think you can accomplish an impossible task, you will come up with a lot of reasons why and how you can make it possible. Start building your critical thinking skills. Stop asking "why?" and start asking "why not?" Or better yet, ask "how?" No matter what you think about a certain situation, you are right. If you think you cannot do it, you will never do it, because chances are you will not even try. If you believe you can, you will persist until you accomplish what it is you set out to do. There are no guarantees in life, except for the belief in yourself. Throughout life, negative people will swarm around you and your dreams, telling you all the reasons why you should take the easy way out and do what society says. If you are crazy enough to believe you can change the world, you will change the world! If you believe you will create a tele-porter, you will create a tele-porter.

What do I believe I will never achieve? Why?
From what I wrote above, give five or more reasons why it is possible!
If I had unlimited resources, what would be my first three steps?

I am not a product of my circumstances. I am a product of my decisions.
~ Stephen R. Covey ~

There will always be circumstances and events in your life you cannot control. You cannot control the weather, natural disasters, media, politics, or people. You can, however, control the thoughts you have and the decisions you make after a circumstance is presented in your life. All the decisions you make create the "product" that is you today. The thoughts you have in your mind determine the decisions you will make when you are faced with any life event. Do not let the events of your life control you. The only things you should be concerned with are your thoughts and actions. This is what makes you who you are! Start making better decisions every moment of every day. Forget the external events in your life, and start living the life of your decisions, because you already are.

What is the "product" I want to become?
What decisions will I be faced with? (List all I can think of)
What are the thoughts and actions of my ideal "product"?

Remember that not getting what you want is sometimes a wonderful stroke of luck.
~ Dalai Lama ~

You've probably experienced this more times than you would have liked, you cannot always get what you want. True! When you do not get what you want, when you hit a brick wall (an obstacle), it has the potential to make you stronger, and put you in another direction which will benefit you more. You may feel like you hit rock bottom when you do not get what you want; feel lucky, because in the end, it can be perceived as a positive. Believe that only good will come from any situation, and good comes—from even the worst situations. Do not live a greedy, envious life, because you will never be satisfied. People who feel entitled to other people's hard work will never be satisfied, because they will always want more of what they do not deserve. As long as you remember you cannot get everything you want, you will be happier. You can try to get everything you want, but when it does not happen, do not give up. You will be pointed in a different direction, with new and better opportunities than what you originally wanted.

> What great thing happened afterI did not get what I originally wanted?
> How did I make that a positive?
> How can I turn an old stroke of bad luck into a positive?

I attribute my success to this: I never gave or took any excuse.
- Florence Nightingale -

Excuses are what our society enables. Give excuses, blame someone else, and complain about the results. Excuses come from the tongues of losers. Start taking responsibility for your actions and your life as a whole. Rationalizing why you did not do something or filing a lawsuit is a lot easier than taking responsibility and blaming yourself. When you own up to your actions, and do not justify your actions, people will notice and look up to you. Most importantly, when you take responsibility for your actions, your subconscious mind will notice. This is very important! When you place blame on others, subconsciously you are giving them control of your life, and you allow life to happen to you. Having bad things happen to you your whole life can force you to see yourself as the victim. A victim is simply a state of mind which you choose. Stop doing that to yourself and take responsibility for your life. No one cares if you are the victim, they are too worried about becoming one themselves. Stop making excuses, and take control of your life. Create your life by taking responsibility!

> What do I think when people give me excuse after excuse?
> What happened one time when I took full responsibility for my actions?
> How can I take responsibility for something I already made an excuse for?

Things work out best for those who make the best of how things work out.
- John Wooden -

If two people are presented with the same seemingly bad situation, a positive thinker will see an opportunity; a negative, small minded thinker will see failure and think horrible thoughts. Things work out because you make them work. You do this by believing they worked out. Your thoughts are the most controllable choice you have in life. When you make the choice in your mind that things will work out, you exponentially increase the chances that they will work. Even when the worst of the worst happens, as long as you are open to good things, something good will come out of the situation. Candy Lightner is the founder of Mothers Against Drunk Drivers (MADD). She took the terrible situation of her daughter's death and turned that trajectory into something wonderful. If a drunk driver had not killed her daughter, MADD might never have been started, drunk driving laws might still be lenient, and awareness of the dangers of drunk driving may still not be known. MADD has saved an incalculable number of lives. Believe, every time, only good can come from this!

> What has been a blessing in disguise?
> What past terrible situation can I make the best of now? How?
> How can the worst thing work out for the best?

Since most problems are created by our imagination and are thus imaginary, all we need are imaginary solutions.
- Richard Bandler -

What we perceive to be real in our mind is actually 100% false. Our past experiences and thoughts taint our perception of events happening in our lives. A great example of this is during a police investigation. There can be five different witnesses with five different accounts of what happened. Truthfully, if you add up those five witness statements, you may possibly get what actually happened in reality. What we perceive in our minds is our own false reality, it is a world created by your imagination. What matters is what we see and how we perceive it. When you look at life positively, you will see mostly positives. A pessimist can always find negatives in life, even after winning a million dollar lottery. Most of our problems as human beings are a figment of our imagination. To come up with a solution to these "problems", we need to imagine a new way of doing things. Take the challenge to imagine all the good that happens in life, and watch your life transform. You will become happier, healthier and more fulfilled; this is a guarantee.

> What problems am I currently producing?
> How can I view my present circumstances from a different perspective?
> What is the solution I imagined to solve my current problem?

A pessimist sees difficulty in every opportunity. An optimist sees the opportunity in every difficulty.
- Winston Churchill -

A pessimist is a negative person who always blames other people, complains about everything, and makes excuses for their actions. An optimist is someone who sees the best in everything and loves life. You can be either one, it is your choice to make. Being an optimist is simply a state of mind. Your thoughts determine whether you are positive or not. All day long, you are presented with opportunities disguised as difficulties. Instead of looking at something as a problem, think of it as an opportunity. Opportunities come in all shapes and sizes when you least expect it, so be prepared. The greatest opportunity comes from a difficult problem which you chose to look at with a positive mind. Difficulties are not excuses to quit. Depending upon your state of mind, you will see difficulties as your time to shine, or as an excuse to quit. They can be difficult to make the most of at times. Remember, everything worthwhile is not easy and everything you are presented with is an opportunity.

How can I make my current problem into an opportunity?
What difficulties was I presented with in the past which I could have looked at as an opportunity?
How can I maximize my next difficulty and make it an opportunity?

Change your thoughts and you change your world.
- Norman Vincent Peale -

Your thoughts make your reality. Everyone does this; do not think you are any different. Your thoughts guide your actions, and your actions produce the results you live. Everything you have in your life, right now, came from your thinking and your thinking alone. All that separates us from each other are our thoughts and actions. On the outside, we are all the same, just another person. What separates the wealthy from the poor are their thought patterns. That is what makes us individuals! They come from years of experience and repetitious phrases getting drilled into us from a young age. You can change your thinking before you even finish reading this sentence; it is your decision to make. Start filling your head with positivity: turn off the TV, stop reading and watching the news. Instead, read self-help books, repeat affirmations, listen to positive audio recordings, and surround yourself with positive people. Figure out who you want to be, determine the thoughts your future self has, and start applying them, today!

What are the three changes I will focus on for the next 18 months?
What thoughts does my future self have on a daily basis?
What thoughts do I need to change to make the above my reality?

We see things not as they are, but as we are.
- Henry Tomlinson -

Perception is interpretation! All the experiences we have in life gave us a particular thought process directly affecting how we see and interpret things. For any situation, each participant will have a unique view. Pessimists will find all the bad things. Optimists will see the good and find a way to make it benefit them. Your thought process determines how you see things; it is not reality. No one sees anything as it really is, it is always colored by our past experiences and thoughts. By changing your thoughts to that of a successful person, you will see the best in every situation, not the worst. To be lucky, you must feel lucky, see lucky, and live lucky. Millions of people a year get diagnosed with a life-changing illness; some see how it can benefit themselves and others, while some wallow in despair to the point of death. A positive mind will produce a long, healthy, positive life! The choice is simple and is yours to make.

What has my perception been over the last thirty days?
What would I like it to be over the next thirty days?
What experience(s) from my past do I think about most often? Why?
What do my current thoughts resemble?
What do I want them to be?

Age is an issue of mind over matter. If you don't mind, it doesn't matter.
- Mark Twain -

Teenagers can accomplish what a seasoned veteran cannot. A senior citizen can accomplish what someone in his or her prime cannot. Age never will matter; the only thing that matters are the thoughts in your mind. There will be some people who look at age as a limitation. Those who are fifteen can accomplish more than someone in their forties. Someone in his or her late nineties can go out and accomplish something that a teenager or middle-aged adult could never do. The saying "mind over matter" is so true. "If you don't mind, it does not matter." You are only as old or as young as you think you are. Age is only a limitation if you let it be. Who is to say what the perfect age is? No one! We all age. The oldest people in the world still learn on a daily basis, so, what is stopping you from achieving greatness? Age has never been, nor will ever be, a valid excuse!

At what age will I be successful?
How did I come up with that conclusion?
How is my age an asset?
What will I tell people who look at my age as a limitation?

It is the mark of an educated mind to be able to entertain a thought without accepting it.
- Aristotle -

You do not have to believe everything you hear, nor do you have to accept it. This means that by being a critical thinker, you can think of plausible ways for something to be true, relevant, or worthwhile to understand it. Can you come up with twenty reasons why Adolf Hitler was a great person? Try it! Entertain this notion since he is considered an egomaniacal racist and the worst genocidal mass murderer the world has ever seen. You do not have to accept it, but it is possible for you to come up with more than fifty reasons. This is an important skill to have in life, for it allows you to understand and appreciate other peoples' points of view. You will then be able to easily sympathize with them. Everyone in the world has a different perspective on everything; if you can entertain their opinions without accepting them, you will become a better communicator and be more liked because you will not be pushing your own agenda on everyone else. Your reality is yours, not theirs, so respect other peoples' reality as their own.

Come up with five positive take-a-ways from Adolf Hitler's existence to prove you can entertain any opinionated thought.
How can I remind myself to be more understanding rather than judgmental?
What benefits will I get from asking questions instead of criticizing?

The starting point of all achievement is desire.
- Napoleon Hill -

There is always a beginning and end to everything you do. To achieve anything, you have to have the desire to achieve what you are working toward. When you have desire, you will have the strength and creativity to overcome the obstacles life will throw at you. In Dr. Stephen Covey's best-selling book *The 7 Habits of Highly Effective People*, his second habit is to "Begin With the End In Mind." Picture what you want to achieve—how it will look, how others will benefit, how you will benefit, etc. Developing this one habit will help develop and strengthen your desire to keep moving forward. The stronger your desire, the more likely it is you will start and finish your dream. If you do not desire to acquire an end result, you will never even begin. In your life right now, you are doing what you desire to do whether you believe it or not. If there is no desire, there will be no action to make it reality. You can believe in yourself all you want, but if it is not backed by desire, the likelihood of starting is nonexistent.

What do I desire to achieve?
What does my end result look, feel, and sound like?
How will it benefit others?
How can I start acting on my desires?
What are my first steps?

Believe you can and you're halfway there.
- Theodore Roosevelt -

You will never start something if you do not believe you can do it. Furthermore, you will never start something if you do not suspect you can finish it. The hardest thing to do is to start. To start, you must have confidence in yourself. The second you have that belief, you are halfway there. The major majority of people do not have high expectations for themselves, so they never begin. The only way to begin is to assume you can do something. When you believe you can achieve anything you set your mind to, the hardest part is over. Now it is a simple matter of working at it every day. You are more capable than you think, and you know you can achieve anything you set your mind too. If you need help, ask for it. People love helping other people, but we are all too afraid to ask. Start asking for help; the worst that can happen is they say no. If you have low self-esteem or confidence, start doing tasks that are proven to build these two vital states of mind. Set small goals and celebrate your successes, say affirmations thousands of times a day, eat healthy, exercise, volunteer, get a hobby, write in a journal, read self-help books, and get eight hours of sleep. There are thousands of things you can do to start believing in yourself. Do them even if you are already confident!

What do I want to believe about myself which I currently do not?
What do I believe I am capable of?
How will I build and reinforce the beliefs I have in myself?

If you can dream it, you can achieve it.
- Zig Ziglar -

You have the capacity to turn any dream into reality. If it is your dream, it can become your reality. Dream big! The bigger your dreams, the bigger the accomplishment. Too many people have dreams and ideas, but never try to pursue them. Rise above the rest, and stop being average. Your dreams can come true through hard work and perseverance. The hard work part may be why most people never try to pursue their dreams; they would rather help others make their dreams reality by filling out applications and becoming an employee. Your dream may be to work for someone or some company, there is absolutely nothing wrong with that—go out and achieve it. All our dreams are different, and the end results we produce are all original. One person's dream job is the next person's nightmare. Stop listening to other people's opinions—go out and achieve your dreams! Never settle for the easy way out. If you want something, go get it. You are your own biggest obstacle on your journey to achievement. Get past your limiting beliefs and fears of failure. Do what you know you will love!

What dream have I achieved in the past? How?
What dream am I currently working on achieving?
What are my next steps?
What is the biggest dream I have for my life?
How will I achieve it?

Do not let what you cannot do interfere with what you can do.
- *John Wooden* -
You are not perfect. You cannot do everything, just like others cannot do the things you can do. Everyone is born with gifts and strengths, as well as handicaps and weaknesses. The key is to discover, develop, and use your gifts and strengths while delegating and forgetting about your weaknesses. Not being able to sing, snowboard, sail, or surf does not stop someone from writing a book. Some authors cannot underline all the nouns, verbs, adverbs, or adjectives in a sentence, nor can they properly structure a sentence to please an English teacher. That has not stopped them from writing books or publishing articles. Do not let anyone tell you that you cannot do something because you are not good at it. Artists who have never surfed should not stop themselves from painting a mural of a surfer. You can do so much more than you cannot do. Forget about your handicaps and weaknesses. So you're not a great artist, but you're great with numbers and explaining things. Don't spend your time wishing you could be a better painter. Focus on being better at what you were already born good at. That's where you'll excel in life. Find your abilities and exploit them. Your gifts, talents, and strengths are waiting for you!

What are my core gifts and abilities?
How can I strengthen them?
What do I want to try which I have never tried before?
What are my strengths and talents?
(HINT: Ask family, friends, and StrengthsFinder 2.0)

Life is 10% what happens to us and 90% how we react to it.
~ Charles R. Swindoll ~

We are presented with a multitude of options every day. With each option, we can make only one decision. Each choice closes off many options and opens many more. This cycle repeats endlessly throughout life: situation, options, response. How you respond to the stuff that happens to you opens and closes different paths to your destination. Have you ever thought about something and said, "I would do it differently if I had the chance?" Making decisions based on your values presents millions of options. What life hands you--the situation--is out of your control; how you respond is what is in your control. "Between stimulus and response, there is a space," said Victor Frankl, the psychologist who survived the Nazi death camps. "In that space is our power to choose our response. In that response lies our growth and freedom." How you respond determines your whole life and reality. How you respond is determined by your thoughts. Just because you responded a certain way in the past does not mean you have to keep responding the same way. Everything that happened and your responses brought you to where you are today, right now.

What "reactions" or responses am I proud of which made me who I am?
How can I correct the results of my previous actions which I am not proud of?
How do I want my life to turn out?
What options do I have to make that happen?

Your problem isn't the problem. Your reaction is the problem.
~ Anonymous ~

Everyone is presented with problems in life. The trick is to not look at the problem as a problem, but rather as an opportunity. There will always be events in your life that present themselves as problems, if you let them. Your thoughts will determine if it is a problem you cannot overcome, or an opportunity you can use as a stepping-stone to success. When a problem/opportunity is presented, you have millions of choices. How you respond will determine the outcome you receive; nothing more, nothing less. The biggest conflicts people face come from their reactions to life events. If you want the outcome you are looking for, start acting in a way to manifest those desires. The Cuban missile crisis was a problem, and JFK responded carefully, in a way that would bring peace. Had he acted in a different way, we might still be living with the aftereffects of nuclear war. Make the correct choice with your end results in mind.

What "problems" am I currently facing?
How are those "problems" an opportunity?
What is my best course of action?

There are two primary choices in life: to accept conditions as they exist, or accept the responsibility for changing them.
~ Denis Waitley ~

Jack Canfield is the co-creator of *Chicken Soup for the Soul*. From 1993–2010 the book sold over 500 million copies in forty-three languages worldwide. In his book *The Success Principles*, he introduces the formula E+R=O (Events + Response = Outcome). You are 100% responsible for your life and the outcomes you produce. You cannot control the (E) events in your life, but you can control your (R) responses to every event that happens. You do this by controlling your thoughts, because inevitably, your thoughts control your actions. Your reaction to an outside factor can give you countless (O) outcomes. Every day, you can take your life in a million different directions by how you respond to all the events that happen. You are the only one who controls your life and the outcomes you live with. Control your reaction, control your outcome!

What areas of life do I need to take responsibility in?
What have I accepted in my life which I am not happy with?
What are the thoughts I should have to live in the conditions I choose?

In matters of style, swim with the current; in matters of principle, stand like a rock.
- Anonymous -

Over time, the styles of the human race have changed with the whims of the majority, but our morals and values have stood like a rock since the beginning of time. In every country, and every generation, there are different styles that the majority agrees upon as the norm. The styles in Los Angeles are different than the style in New York. In the city of Milwaukee, the style is different on Brady Street versus Milwaukee Street versus Fond du Lac Avenue. When you go with the current, your style is like everyone else, and changes quickly. Good versus bad morals, along with values, are constantly being debated. They do change, but it takes time for the majority to accept changes. When a rock stands still in a river, erosion takes place, wearing the rock down until it is wiped away by the current—accepted by the majority. Think of the erosion process as strikes, sit-ins, and protests. They are not going to get their way instantly, it takes time for critical mass to take hold. Do not get swept away from your principles!

When have I went against my principles and followed the majority?
What principles are my rocks?
How have I gone against who I am just to be accepted? Why?

A man can be as great as he wants to be. If you believe in yourself and have the courage, the determination, the dedication, the competitive drive and if you are willing to sacrifice the little things in life and pay the price for the things that are worthwhile, it can be done.
- Vince Lombardi -

Any and everything is possible, especially with twenty-first century technology! Think of everything we have now that was considered impossible fifty years ago, or even ten years ago. Do not limit yourself based on what society or people around you say about who you are or who you should be. Believe in yourself and everything you are capable of. To pursue any dream, you need to have the courage to face the negativity that will come. You need determination and dedication to keep going after you fail. You need competitive drive to make it better than anyone else could ever dream. You will need to sacrifice time spent on what you normally do, and dedicate it to who you want to become. There will be a price to pay to become the person you want to be, and create something the world sees as worthwhile. Invest in yourself with positive choices, confident in the worthwhile outcome.

> How great will I become if I stay on the same path?
> How great do I want to become? (Be specific!)
> What am I willing to sacrifice to become great and worthwhile?

Anything I can do, you can do better. It is a matter of belief backed by desire.
- Lucas J. Robak -
You can achieve anything you want to achieve, regardless of your disabilities as long as you believe in yourself and have the desire to make it your reality. If you want to be a rocket scientist, but cannot even add, you can still make it happen, as long as you believe you can do it and have the desire to accomplish it. It will be a lot of work, obviously, but it is more than possible. Having a burning desire is not enough, you must first posses the belief in yourself to make it possible. If a rocket scientist wanted to be a rock star, but never held an instrument, it is perfectly possible for that to happen only if they first believe they can do it, then have the desire to sit and practice for hours on end. They may not have the musical talent, but with belief and a burning desire to obtain that rock star status, it is possible. What is easy for one person can be extremely difficult for the next. As long as you believe you can accomplish something, and if you work hard enough, you will be able to do it better than someone with natural talent. Anything and everything can be learned through practice. Believe you can achieve your desires then go out and make it happen.

> What do I want to be better at?
> What area do I want to known as an expert?
> What do I desire most from life?

No one can make you feel inferior without your consent.
- Eleanor Roosevelt -
Do not allow or give permission to anyone to make you feel low quality, or of less importance. These are your feelings and your life. By choosing to think positively and have feelings of self-worth, you will always be above those who treat you as of little importance. Have a sense of self-worth and treat yourself the way you treat those you love, for you deserve no less. Treat yourself with respect and people will treat you the same. When people talk down to you, and they will, it is up to you to not feel inferior. The feelings you experience are 100% your responsibility; they come from your own thinking. The second someone makes you feel inferior is the second you consented for that to happen. Treat yourself the way you treat your most treasured possessions, and you will live a life of quality.

When was the last time I felt inferior?
How did I allow that to happen?
What are my great qualities which give me worth? (HINT: Ask friends and family)
How will I react next time someone tries to make me feel inferior?

The mind is everything. What you think, you become.
- Buddha -

Your thoughts dictate your actions. Your actions, accumulated over a period of time, determine what your reality is. If you have thoughts of love and positivity, your actions will follow suit and you will become a respectable human being who people admire. If you have thoughts of fear and negativity, likewise, your actions will follow suit and you will become lonely and despised by others. You can control your thoughts by thinking about thinking. Be conscious of your thoughts, and in time, it will become habit to think thoughts of abundance, or whatever it is that you choose. Determine who you want to become, and research the thoughts those kinds of people have. Make those thoughts your core focus until they are habit! Become the person you want to become simply by thinking. Indeed, thoughts are things!

Who do I want to become?
What thoughts do I need to eliminate from my mind?
What thoughts do I need to have?

You can run from your problems but not from the flaws in your thinking. Always start by fixing your brain. Train it to remove logical fallacies.
- Tai Lopez -

You have a perception of the world, it is yours and yours alone. Your internal image of your problems will be impossible to overcome until you change your thinking. This is as easy as making the choice to change your thinking, or as hard as living your whole life and realizing on your deathbed that it was not difficult at all. A real difficulty is only as hard as you make it. If you think everything is easy, it will be. The hardest of tasks can be broken down into a lot of action steps so they are not as difficult. It is as simple as that. A real difficulty will take more thinking, time, and action steps over something easy. The only thing holding you back is your limiting beliefs about yourself and all the fallacies you were raised to believe. Your imagination can be your worst enemy or your greatest asset. Stop turning your thoughts against yourself and conquer your dreams!

What have I given up on because of the false limiting beliefs my parents, teachers, coaches, and friends projected upon me?
What imaginary difficulties do I face on a daily basis?
How can I overcome my current difficult situation?

Too many of us are not living our dreams because we are living our fears.
~ Les Brown ~

Fear is the root of all failure. Fear is what stops us from trying or moving forward in difficult times. We live in fear on a day-to-day basis. Instead of moving toward our goals, we move away from our fears. It is a catch-22, because our goals lie deep within our fears. To accomplish any worthwhile goal, you have to face your fears and step out of your comfort zone. There is a way around never facing your fears: never set any goals, live an unaccomplished life, allow circumstances and other people to control every aspect of your life, and be miserable. —OR— Place your fears in front of you, defeat them by facing them, and thrive within them. For every fear you have, there are millions of people who live with it every day. Those same people have their own fears which millions of others live with. Fear is a state of mind which you can overcome through repetition. Constantly face your fears, and they will no longer keep you from living your dreams!

What fears am I living in?
What fears do I need to get over in order for me to live my dreams?
What can I realistically do to ease myself into being comfortable with my fears?

When one door of happiness closes, another opens, but often we look so long at the closed door that we do not see the one that has been opened for us.
~ Helen Keller ~

The past is the past; get over it and move on. Too often we dwell on the past when we lose something or someone, and that blinds us to all the opportunities that continue to appear. Time will move on, with or without us. No matter how good or bad we feel, the sun will still rise tomorrow. "For every door that closes, one more opens" is a potent truth. Truly believe that for every door that closes, an entire floor of doors open. Opportunities and choices are endless. Once one door closes, you no longer have that possibility blinding you from seeing what is behind the next ten thousand doors. When a door closes on you, that moment is your opportunity. You can look at the door, but do not have to walk through it. Meaning, be open to and see what opportunities are out there for you. Choose the ones you want.

What opportunities do I have available to me right now?
What are the greatest benefits I will receive from going through that newly opened door?
What opportunities do I want available to me in the near future?
How will I create them?

I am always doing that which I cannot do, in order that I may learn how to do it.
~ Pablo Picasso ~

No matter what the field, even the most talented people did not know how to do it at one point. Computer programmers could not program anything until they learned how. A great leader did not just pop up from out of nowhere, they learned how to do what they do. You can learn anything and everything you want to. The only thing holding you back is you. There are many options when it comes to learning something new. You can teach yourself through reading, YouTube, and most importantly by doing it. You can learn from those who have already accomplished what you want to learn, through lessons, seminars, workshops, and books. You can learn more by doing than you ever would by sitting in a classroom for decades. True mastery comes from practice, not from being lectured. You cannot learn how to play a guitar by studying music, you learn by playing the instrument. You do not need knowledge to do things, you simply need to start doing it!

What have I learned from doing?
(Not walking, talking, reading, the bathroom, and using a cell phone)
What do I want to learn to do? (List everything that comes to mind)
How am I able to learn what I want to learn?
What do I need to do to acquire this knowledge?

Don't let the fear of losing be greater than the excitement of winning.
- Robert Kiyosaki -
Most people develop the fear of losing, and lose sight of what can be gained. When a sports team takes the field, they are excited about the win and what that will bring, rather than not showing up because they fear losing. Taking risks is scary because of the fear of losing everything. The reason people do risk everything is because of what will be gained when they succeed. This creates billionaires, they risk everything they have and come out on top, usually after numerous attempts and bankruptcies. Robert Kiyosaki is a self-made billionaire and owner of *Rich Dad Education* who at one point lived out of his car. The fear of losing should never hold you back. Start thinking in terms of what can be gained, and you will succeed. It will give you courage and perseverance to get through all the tough times which lie ahead.

What could I lose by taking that risk I am thinking of?
What will I gain from taking that risk?
How will my life be different after winning?

Dream big and dare to fail.
- Norman Vaughan -
The bigger the dream, the bigger the reward. The bigger the reward, the bigger the risk. The bigger the risk, the bigger the fear. When you have a big dream, there is a great chance you will fail—big. Do not let the fear of failure stop you from working toward making your dream a reality. The only way to accomplish anything is by daring failure to stop you. The only way you will fail is the second you decide to give up completely. You may decide one day to give up and the next day to start again; that is not failure because you are still working toward your dream. Dare to fail, and you will succeed. Believe in yourself and have the desire to achieve, and

there will be nothing that can stop you. When you have a dream, an idea, you have that for a reason. It is up to you to make it into reality. Stop thinking someone else will do it; you are that someone else. Face fear and failure head on to achieve your wildest dreams!

What are all of my big dreams?
What is my biggest dream?
What positive outcome can come from accomplishing my biggest dream?

All progress takes place outside the comfort zone.
~ Michael John Bobak ~

Your comfort zone is a very small box which only you live in. However, many people are in this small box of a comfort zone and each person is just as lonely as the next. It is a lonely, over crowded place which allows zero growth. You will constantly be living the same life situations and getting the same results until you step outside of it. When something scares you, do it. When something is outside your comfort zone, do it. Fear is essential to growth and for creating new opportunities. You develop new skills and meet new people when you leave your comfort zone behind. The current life that you have is comfortable to you, but if you stayed there for the rest of your life, would you be satisfied? No, you would potentially feel unfulfilled living the exact same life for decades with zero growth. The only way to make progress in your life is to step outside your comfort zone, face your fears, and make things happen for yourself.

How is my comfort zone limiting me?
What do I want to do which is outside my comfort zone?
What excitement will I experience by doing something that scares me?

No man ever achieved worth-while success who did not, at one time or other, find himself with at least one foot hanging well over the bring of failure.
~ Napoleon Hill ~

To succeed, your desire for the outcome must be stronger than your fears. You might fear failure, success, big crowds, or public speaking. In order to be accomplished, you have to get out of your comfort zone and make things happen. Nothing will ever happen in your comfort zone. Success is what people in their comfort zones watch others have. Courage is grace under pressure of fear; fear remains, it is just the ability to face it. Stop being afraid of things that other people are not afraid of. Make it a point each day to face one of your fears. If you are human, you have a whole list of fears. If something scares you or makes you uncomfortable to think about, do not hesitate, do it!

What's one fear I will need to face?
What can I do to live outside my comfort zone once a day?
What do I need to do to succeed which elicits fear by simply thinking about it?

The road to success and the road to failure are almost exactly the same.
~ Colin R. Davis ~

In life, you can take any road you want and still make it to where you want to go. You can do this by turning around, cutting across fields, or sticking it out to see what happens. The only way you can make any of these diversions to become your road to success is to keep truckin' past all the roadblocks, accidents, and checkpoints. That is the only way you will succeed. The same road many people are on has potential to lead each vehicle to a different destination. When you come to intersections and bypasses—your daily choices—you can go in millions of directions. There will be times when it appears you are headed in the wrong direction because of the failures you encounter, but by staying on that same road, all those failures will take you to your destination of success.

When did I think I was failing, but then succeeded?
What direction have I decided to take as my life's destination?
What is the worst that can happen when I persevere through my failures?

Many of life's failures are experienced by people who did not realize how close they were to success when they gave up.
~ Thomas Edison ~

People give up far too easily. Many give up just before success takes hold. Success is always one more try away. If you keep giving it one more try, you will succeed. It is a universal law! Success comes to those who do not quit. It is hard for someone to fail if they never give up. You will never know how close you are to success until you become a success. Failure is giving up, quitting. You will never be a success if you stop trying when it could have been one more try away. Also, look at who said this quote—Thomas Edison. It took Thomas Edison ten thousand tries to make a light bulb. We would still be living with oil lamps and candles if he had given up at try 9,999. He experimented ten thousand times, and changed the world.

What did I give up on before I succeeded?
What would my world be like if I kept trying until I succeeded?
What should I give 10,000 more tries at success?

Develop success from failures. Discouragement and failure are two of the surest stepping stones to success.
~ Dale Carnegie ~

You will fail! This is a guarantee in life; there is no way around it other than to never try at all. Each failure you encounter opens up more opportunities and is a great learning experience. Learn what you did right, what you did wrong, and how you can do it differently the next time around. When you do it again, take note of what went right and what went wrong, whether or not you succeeded. There is huge potential in learning from your successes. You will never do something with absolute perfection, there will always be room for improvement. When you fail, you may experience symptoms such as dismay, depression, moping around, pessimism, and you end up giving up. These feelings are a part of the natural process on your journey to success, anyone worth mentioning went through it at some point many times. Keep experimenting, and you will succeed.

What was my greatest failure?
What did I learn?
What made me experience one, or all, of the symptoms of failure?
What did I learn from my failures?
How can I do it differently next time?

An obstacle is often a stepping-stone.
~ William Prescott ~

When you climb stairs, each step helps you get to the next one. All are necessary to get to the top. Every hardship in your life will help you grow and take you to the next obstacle. Add up all the difficulties, build a staircase with them, and get to where you are going. Hurdles are a necessary part of the process by helping you develop the skills necessary to build you as a person. All the stairs you climb help build your muscles so you can keep climbing every staircase you want. Doing stair exercises is a great workout and helps you stay in shape, the same goes for obstacles. Every bump makes you stronger and helps you get closer to your destination. They are a great way to learn new skills, meet new people, and face your fears so you grow as an individual. If there were no obstacles, this would be a perfect world and everyone would get what they wanted. Thankfully, that is not the case; you have to work for what you want, and persist through the hard times. Life is never easy, and it never will be. However, it is easy to get jealous and demand you have the right to other people's success; it is hard to go out and become a success yourself. Get past the stumbling blocks and succeed in life.

What obstacles helped put me in the direction of something better?
What learning came from my obstacles?
What skills have I developed because of an obstacle?

A person who never made a mistake never tried anything new.
~ Albert Einstein ~

The only way to learn something new is through making mistakes. Even if you did all your homework and acquired all the knowledge you need, miscalculations will still be made. When you actually do something, you learn more in that one attempt than from decades of studying, reading, and being in a classroom. You will make mistakes, and you probably will fail more times than you would like. That is a part of the learning process. Learn by doing! Learn by failing! Learn by making mistakes! Learn through risk taking! Learn through repetition! Get off your butt and make as many mistakes as you possibly can, learn from them, then get out there and do it again differently with your new knowledge. Continue this process tens of thousands of times until you produce the results you want.

What new things have I tried recently?
What did I learn from my mistakes?
What new things am I thinking about trying?
What am I waiting for?
What mistakes will I make in the future?
What can I do to avoid them?

Every strike brings me closer to the next home run.
~ Babe Ruth ~

In his career, Babe Ruth had 714 home runs and struck out 1,330 times. Each strikeout means he saw three pitches, minimum, each time he was at bat. So Babe Ruth saw, at minimum, 3,990 strikes thrown at him in order to hit those 714 home runs; that's an 18% success rate. If each strike is seen by Babe Ruth as a failure, and each home run a success, he failed over five-and-a-half times more than he succeeded. In life, most people do not even attempt to go to the plate out of fear of failure, and never see one pitch. To truly succeed, you will have to fail more times than you succeed. The public does not see the failures, they see the success that may take decades to manifest into reality. All those failures will make you into a successful person! True winners are the ones who make the most errors. We remember Babe Ruth as a baseball legend, not the strike-out king.

In the past, how many times did I fail before I succeeded?
What is my most recent "strike" which brought me closer to my next "home run"?
What am I trying to achieve this week/month/year/decade?

Great minds discuss ideas. Average minds discuss events. Small minds discuss people.
~ Henry Thomas Buckle ~

Think about the people who surround you. You are the average of the five people you hang out with most. What do you talk about? Ideas turn into reality; events are things of the past; people are not worth discussing, because gossip has no value. When you hear people talk about ideas and all the possibilities life has to offer, it is exciting, even for those who just listen in. When people talk about events of the past, they are talking about something they cannot control, and no longer matters. When you talk about people, it is usually complaining about them—pure negativity. When you discuss ideas, you are inspiring yourself and others. Look around right now and notice what is around you. Everything you see started out as a dream. If it wasn't for someone turning his or her idea into reality, you would have nothing in your life but wilderness. Become that great thinker you were meant to be by surrounding yourself with big thinkers and isolating the small-minded dream stealers of your life.

What do I find myself normally discussing?
How do I feel after those conversations?

What is one statement or question I can ask to turn a small-minded or average conversation into one that great minds have?
What are five things I can do to start having conversations about ideas more often?

Great spirits have always encountered violent opposition from mediocre minds.
- Albert Einstein -

Immediately after the above, Einstein wrote in his letter to Morris Raphael Cohen, "The mediocre mind is incapable of understanding the man who refuses to bow blindly to conventional prejudices and chooses instead to express his opinions courageously and honestly." When you have a new idea, you will encounter conflict from small-minded thinkers who are set in their ways; these same small-minded people will be the first to say, "have an open mind" or "think out of the box". Once you are able to deal with conflict confidently, tactfully and maturely, you can get past all of life's negativity. You may even win some negative people to your side. When people do not agree with you, their words, and sometimes their actions, become violent so as to silence you and make you give up. Learn how to deal with conflict, and you will succeed!

How do I currently deal with conflict?
How has it been working for me?
What have I given up because of conflict with a mediocre, average, or small mind?
What are my options to avoid the small, mediocre minds of my life?

The person who says it cannot be done should not interrupt the person who is doing it.
- Chinese Proverb -

A dream stealer is someone who gave up on his or her dreams, and wants to get you to give up on yours. They are the ones who tried, failed, and gave up. In their minds it cannot be done, so they want everyone who is still trying to know that it is impossible. A dream stealer is someone who does not have any critical thinking skills; they are small thinkers. These small-minded people do not see the big picture of what could be. Rather, they see all the things that could go wrong, and all the reasons why one should not even try. A small-minded person does not believe in himself or herself enough to believe in anyone else. They are the ones who gave up and put themselves on the sidelines to watch everyone else succeed, while they boo, taunt, and try to bring everyone else down. Unless a dream stealer's effort inspires you to succeed, these people are irrelevant, and you need to ignore their attempts to steal your dream. You may even kick them completely out of your life if you want.

What did I accomplish after a dream stealer told me it could not be done?
What am I working on that I was told was impossible?

What is something that I believe to be impossible, but is something I want to accomplish?

There are two types of people who will tell you that you cannot make a difference in this world: those who are afraid to try themselves, and those who are afraid you will succeed.
~ Ray Goforth ~

Many call them dream stealers. You will encounter dream stealers at every turn in life, from the day you are born until the day you die. The most important thing to remember is that these people and their opinions are completely irrelevant to you and your dreams. They chose to develop the victim mindset because they too encountered others who stole their dreams. They were too afraid to try or try again, and they gave up. They will tell you it is impossible or stupid. They may be filled with jealousy, envy, and bitterness. Unconsciously, they do not want people to succeed because they want to keep others at their level. Small minds, negative people, and dream stealers bring people down; winners help others succeed and are happy when they do. Look for the winners in life. When you come across a dream stealer—and you will—remember: their opinions are irrelevant to your passions and purpose.

Who are the dream stealers in my life?
What dreams have I given up on because of a dream stealer?
What dreams do I want to pursue again?
How will I steal back my dreams and ignore the dream stealers?

The number one reason people fail in life is because they listen to their friends, family, and neighbors.
~ Napoleon Hill ~

Beginning in childhood, we are told what to do, what to think, and how to act. Who we are today is a result of the environments we grew up in. If you take a child born in Milwaukee, Wisconsin, and raise it in Nanjin, China, the chance of that child being able to speak English is small. As we get older, the people in our lives can still determine what we become, because we allow it to happen. Your family, friends, teachers, coaches, and neighbors are the people most able to discourage you from pursuing your dreams. But only if you allow it. If you share an idea you have with one of them, they may try to talk you out of it because it is not their dream for themselves or for you, or because they do not believe in themselves. You are your own person, and you have the potential to achieve anything you want in life. Stop listening to other people, and start listening to yourself!

What goal has the negativity of my friends, family, teachers, and/or neighbors held me back from?
In what areas of my life do I need to stop listening to these people?
Who do I need to kick out of my life because of their negativity?
How will I tactfully do it?

There is only one way to avoid criticism: do nothing, say nothing, and be nothing.
- Elbert Hubbarb -

There are always trolls out there who will criticize what you do and/or how you do it. The only way to avoid criticism is to never try. Those with ideas and dreams are often the ones who get criticized the most. When you do nothing, you will accomplish nothing. When you say nothing, you will not be heard, and you allow other people to control your circumstances. Doing nothing brings nothing. When someone criticizes you, it is feedback you are doing something right. You will never be able to please everyone, and if you do, you are definitely doing something wrong. When you receive criticism, turn it into constructive criticism because you are on the right path for yourself!

What criticism do I regularly receive?
How can I make it constructive to my goals?
What criticism am I actively avoiding?
What harm is that doing?
What is the best that can happen for me when I stop avoiding and give up my fear of criticism?

Whatever the mind can conceive and believe, the mind can achieve.
- Napoleon Hill -

This quote is written numerous times throughout Napoleon Hill's best-selling book, *Think and Grow Rich*. If you have not already, Read that book! The book is a collection of wisdom garnered from studying the lives and behavior of extremely successful people for twenty years. Published in 1937, the classic book reveals this universal truth, which he observed in all successful people. Whatever idea your mind can come up with, as long as you believe it possible, you will be able to make it a reality. This does not mean it will be an easy process, or that your idea will be reality within a day or even a decade. It means you have the power to create anything your mind imagines. Everything we have today all started out as a simple idea, backed by years of hard work, determination, and perseverance. Your dreams, ideas, and imagination are your most valuable assets; treat them as such. Believe in yourself, and you will accomplish unbelievably incredible dreams. Millions who started out just like you already have, and you can, too.

What ideas do I have which I would like to see become reality?
What do I believe I can possibly achieve in this lifetime?
What would I like to achieve but do not believe I can at this moment?

You measure the size of the accomplishment by the obstacles you had to overcome to reach your goals.
- Booker T. Washington -

Creating a goal and succeeding is not about what you gain from the results, but rather who you become along the way. It is what you learn, the skills you acquire, the obstacles you overcome, and who you become as a person. The tougher the obstacles, the bigger the accomplishments. Think in terms of traveling. One goal is to walk to the grocery store and back. The obstacles you might face are stairs, doors, traffic, traffic lights, people, and a line. Another goal is to get to the other side of the country, with no money, within three days. Think of those obstacles you will have to overcome. The level of difficulty in the task will directly affect your satisfaction and feeling of accomplishment. Granted, not everyone can walk to the grocery store, and some people may consider that as one of their biggest accomplishments. Everyone is different in their own deserving right.

>What are the biggest obstacles I am currently facing?
>What accomplishment do I need to achieve so I can say, "This is the biggest accomplishment of my life?"
>What will happen if I don't get it?
>What won't happen if I do get it?

The successful warrior is the average man, with laser-like focus.
- Bruce Lee -

We are all one in the same. The only thing that separates us from each other is our thoughts. Focus falls into this category. To have laser-like focus is to ignore all distractions around us. Technically speaking, we are all average people, some more focused than others. Focus comes from desire and passion to finish a task or project. Whether assigned or started on your own, it is the passion and desire that gives you the focus you need to ignore all distractions and successfully complete the task. As people, we all have the same decision to make, choose to create a bunch of lame excuses and reasons to cry out on the mountain top, or we can choose to produce results. What's better, creating reasons or creating results?

>What do I do which gives me the most focus?
>What distractions can I eliminate when working on accomplishing something?
>(HINT: Technology)
>What time of day do I get the most work done?

To accomplish great things; we must not only act, but also dream; not only plan, but also believe.
- Anatole France -

All achievements begin as an idea from one's imagination. Whether it is from the creative imagination (completely original) or the synthetic imagination (using what has already been created to make something new), all accomplishments start out as just a dream, an idea, a vision. Motivation comes from the daily belief in oneself to be able to manifest the idea. A great plan or goal does not need to be detailed or elaborate. Goals and plans change as you learn. The only way to learn is to start acting on your plan, your dream. Through the simple act of doing, taking action, you will open up more opportunities and learn more than just simply reading a book and listening to a lecture. Get out there and make it happen!

What is a dream I have for myself?
What will happen when I get it?
What resources will I use to get it?

If you don't design your own life plan, chances are you'll fall into someone else's plan. And guess what they have planned for you? Not much.
~ Jim Rohn ~

If you do not know where you are going, you will not know which way to turn or even when you arrive. When you drive to school or work, you know where you are starting from and where your destination is. On your way there, you know when and where to turn. You are even able to take different routes if there is an accident or a traffic jam. Also, you clearly know when you arrive. However, if you are falling into someone else's plan, who has nothing planned for you, you may not even be able to find your car. That "someone else" took your car because you going to where you needed to be was not a part of their plan. There are a lot of bosses out there who only think about themselves and their goals because they are the ones paying you to create their dream, not your dream. If you getting to work was not a part of that plan, there is nothing to stop them from taking your car. This is why goals for yourself is so important. Take control of your life and make a plan for where you want to go! Chances are, people will bend over backwards to help you along the way!

What plan am I a part of that is not mine?
How can I change that?
What is the life I want to live?
What plan do I need to implement for it happen?
What resources do I currently have which will assist me?
What resources do I need to acquire?

**The reason most people never reach their goals is that they don't define them, or ever seriously consider them as believable or achievable. Winners can tell you where they are going, what they plan to do along the way, and who will be sharing
the adventure with them.**
~ Denis Waitley ~

(S) is a balance between Specific and Simple. Make it easy enough for a 5-year-old child to tell others and to let you know how close you are to achieving it if you haven't already.

(M) is to make it Meaningful to you. Pursuing this has to be your choice which supports your purpose.

(A) has two meanings: the goal should address All Areas of your life, and be written As if it is your current reality. With anything in life, your goals should ideally be in harmony with your values, principles, and the six areas of life (Career/School, Health & Fitness, Relationships, Family, Personal Development, and Spiritual Growth).

(R) is to determine if the goal is **Responsible and Ecological**. Think about the consequences, both good and bad, of achieving your goal for yourself and the world around you.

(T) is to make sure you are going **T**oward what you want by a certain **T**ime. When setting a deadline, it is always a guess!

>**Specifically Simple:**
>What is my specific and simple goal?
>How is it measurable?
>**Meaningful:**
>What does obtaining this goal mean for me?
>For what purpose do I want it?
>**All Areas** of your life, written **As if** is a reality now:
>What areas of my life are impacted
>by the achievement of this goal?
>**Responsible & Ecological:**
>What are the consequences, both good and bad,
>of achieving the goal for myself and the world?
>**Toward** what you want by what **Time**:
>By when will this goal be completed?
>Verify you're moving towards, not away from something.

The trouble with not having a goal is that you can spend your life running up and down the field and never score.
>*- Bill Copeland -*

A goal is a destination. In basketball it is the hoop; in soccer, hockey, lacrosse, etc. it is the net; football and rugby it is the end zone. Athletes know exactly where they need to end up to win. Life is the same way. If you do not have a goal, how will you know you achieved anything? When you do not know where you are going—in sports, driving, life in general—you will aim mindlessly and never actually know if you succeeded. Have a goal and know where you are going! It boosts self-esteem and gives your life direction.

>What are five outcomes I want to achieve?
>What is my start and finish date?
>What are five outcomes I want to achieve in the next ninety days?
>What is my start and finish date?
>What will not happen if I achieve this?
>How will my life change when I achieve this?

All our dreams can come true—if we have the courage to pursue them.
>*- Walt Disney -*

The number one thing that holds most people back from starting anything is fear. Fear of failure, fear of success, fear of ridicule, and so on. Believe that you can live the life you dream of. Everything starts out as just a dream, and we can benefit from other people's courage to overcome the obstacles life throws at us. Courage is nothing more than looking at failure as feedback, rather than a reason to give up and let someone else achieve your dream! Courage is a state of mind that you can develop over time. Walt Disney was fired from a job because he was told he had no imagination. That did not stop him from taking action and creating a global empire.

Which of my dreams have I not pursued, yet?
How will the community benefit from the completion of my dream?
Who do I need to look to for the courage to proceed?

Vision without action is a daydream. Action without vision is a nightmare.
~ Japanese Proverb ~

Everything we have in life started out as an idea, a vision. We all have them every day. The only way to turn your vision into reality is through action and perseverance. If you do not act on your ideas, they will never manifest themselves. "No one will do your push-ups for you." The opposite end of the spectrum is acting when you have no vision. This is not a good thing either because if you have no vision, goal, or end in mind, you have no direction. When you do not have direction, you will not know what to do next, or even why you are doing something. A vision, coupled with action, is essential to success. With no action, your dream will never be a reality. With no vision, you go through the motions without direction.

What happened when I started doing something before thinking about how to accomplish it?
What vision have I yet to take action on?
What are my first action steps to make my vision a reality?

The journey of a thousand miles begins with one step.
~ Lao Tzu ~

Everything starts somewhere. You cannot start a project from the middle. There will always be a beginning, middle, and end. When you go on a road trip, it starts even before you pack your bags: you make plans. When you begin driving, you have a starting point. Think of a big goal laid out before you as a trip of a thousand miles. For each mile in that journey, there are thousands of steps you need to take. You cannot take those steps until you start. You do not need to know all the directions and all the steps before you start; all you need to do is start. How you start really is not that big of a deal. As long as you start, you will begin to see what you should do to put yourself on the right path. Start! Take action today!

What is one desire that I want to be reality?
What do I think are my first few steps?
What will I regret if I do not take these first steps?

The best time to plant a tree was twenty years ago. The second best time is now.
- Chinese Proverb -

All you have is your immediate present to do something. If you used your immediate present a year ago to take action, your life would be drastically different than it is now. Do not dwell on the past! Do not regret not having done something because that will inhibit you from moving forward. Take action now: your immediate present is the only time you will ever have to change your life. Nothing will happen without you taking action in your present moment. Make up for lost time, and use everything you learned over the course of your inaction to be successful now. If you passed up an opportunity before, do not dwell on it. Instead, create that opportunity again. Make it happen. Reap the benefits, and live it up!

What did I not start before which I wish I had?
What are the benefits I would be receiving if I had taken action?
What can I do now to take action so that I will live those benefits?

It is never too late to be what you might have been.
- George Eliot -

If you had followed through on something you gave up on, you would already be living the benefits. Do not get discouraged, the great thing about life is that it is never too late to start again. Even if you are in your eighties, you can achieve the life you wanted when you were in your twenties. Some limitations apply, but that should not stop you. The only time you fail is when you give up completely. It may take decades to come back to your original plan, but this is your second chance. Achieve the life you've always wanted!

What dream have I given up on but is still in my mind?
What does the final outcome look, feel, and sound like?
What are the first three action steps I will take this week?

Good things come to people who wait, but better things come to those who go out and get them.
- Anonymous -

Patience is a virtue, but what is even better is taking the initiative. If you sit and wait around for something great to happen to you, the chances are not good. If you go out and work to make something great happen, your chances increase drastically. When you think in terms of patience, think about when you are making things happen. There are times when being patient is better than taking the initiative. For instance, when you present an offer and they say they will call you next week, do not call them the next day. Wait until next week when it is appropriate to take the initiative again. You must build the skill of knowing when to wait and when to take action. Taking action beats patience nine times out of ten. Good things will come to those who wait, but only after taking action to earn that opportunity to practice patience.

How did I receive something great from patience?
What were my actions which lead up to that?
How did I receive something great from taking action? What did I do?
What do I need to be more patient with?
What do I need to take action on?

You miss 100% of the shots you don't take.
~ Wayne Gretzky ~

The answer to every question you do not ask will always be no. How can you score a goal in hockey if you never shoot? You have to take chances. You have to take risks. You have to get comfortable going out of your comfort zone. Taking those shots you have never taken before will be uncomfortable at first, but like anything, in time, it will become second nature to take the shots you know you should take. Get comfortable with asking the so-called stupid questions; you never know what opportunities may present themselves. Think in terms of action, now. Every time you do not go out and take a shot at an idea you have, it will never happen. You will never get a job unless you take a shot and apply. You will never date unless you take a shot and ask them out. Take that shot. Now!

What stopped me from taking that "shot" I am still thinking about?
What "shot" have I not taken which I will take this week?
What is the worst that could happen if I miss after taking the "shot"?

Don't be afraid to give up the good to go for the great.
~ John D. Rockefeller ~

When you go for the greatness life has to offer, you will be risking everything that you know right now. You will either fail and lose everything, or you could become one of the most successful people the world has seen. It is good to be in a safe career with benefits, but it is great to create your own job, hire employees, and be an important part in supporting many families. It is good to live your life the way society dictates; it is great to go against the norm and become successful. Being good is simply average. Anyone can experience something good. Only those who risk and sacrifice are the ones who become great. Greatness is something the majority of people fail to even attempt once, though we all want it. The great become great because they go out and do great things with their great ideas for decades until they become a global reality.

What greatness am I living right now?
What greatness do I want to achieve?
What good things will I give up to become great?
(TV, video games, cell phone, fiction books, etc. included!)

Even if you're on the right track, you'll get run over if you just sit there.
~ Will Rogers ~

Every day we are presented with millions of different choices. You may already be making all the right decisions which put you on the right track. If you do not take action every day, or at a minimum every week, you will get passed up by other people who are diligently working hard when you are out with your friends. No matter what you are working on, someone somewhere is doing what you are trying to do. If you sit idly by, they will run you over and be the successful one. Every day, do one thing that will take you closer to your desired outcome; do ten things if you can. There are numerous distractions that will get you run over by others: TV, news, video games, social media, drinking, drugs, laziness, procrastination, celebrity pop news, holidays, weekends, politics, and more. Start eliminating the junk from your life, and make time for success!

What junk do I waste my potential on?
What time wasters can I eliminate out of my life?
What can I work on instead of just "sitting on the tracks"?

If you can breathe, you can achieve!
~ Lucas J. Robak ~

If you breathe, you are alive. If you are alive, there is nothing stopping you from achieving—except for you. There will be obstacles along the way that will prevent you from easily accomplishing what you are pursuing, but that is what is great about life. When you hit obstacles, your thinking gets stretched, and your horizons expand in order to achieve the outcome you desire. To achieve all of your wildest dreams, it is as simple as believing in yourself. Once you believe you can do it, the next step is to do it. Start, and see it through to the end. In achieving the outcome, your greatest accomplishment will be what you learned along the way. Yes, your outcome will become reality, but the most important part is who you become on the path to success. You will be stronger, smarter, and more creative than before.

What have I achieved in the past which I am proud of?
What do I need to do differently to achieve what I am currently working on?
What would I like to achieve in the future which I haven't started yet?
What are my first three steps?

In any situation, the best thing you can do is the right thing; the next best thing you can do is the wrong thing; the worst thing you can do is nothing.
~ Theodore Roosevelt ~

By doing nothing, you will get nothing. By doing the wrong thing, you at least did something, and were able to learn from it. Obviously, doing the right thing is best in any situation. To know what is right in every situation is easier than you think; follow your instincts and conscience. If you feel like something is wrong, do not do it. When some problem arises, you have three options: do the right thing, do the wrong thing, or do nothing. When you do nothing, you are allowing life to control what happens to you. In doing so, you have no say in what happens to your life and you now have zero right to complain about anything. When you do what is right, or even wrong, you are at least taking back control of your life. No matter what happens and what you do, learn from what led up to that situation, and what happened when you took action. Learn from the feedback life hands you and grow as a person.

> What happened after I did not take action?
> Am I happy with those results?
> In a situation where I did what was right, how did I know that was the right thing to do?
> When I did the wrong thing in a situation that called for action, what did I learn from the results?
> How will I do it differently when I create that chance again?

It does not matter how slowly you go as long as you do not stop.
~ Confucius ~

If you start in Milwaukee, Wisconsin, and every day you take one step south, then sit down until the next day when you do it again, you cannot deny that one day you will end up in Chicago, Illinois. You could also choose to take five or ten steps a day; or three a week. You will eventually make it to your destination, as long as you do not stop. The same applies to anything you are trying to accomplish in life. Take three steps toward your goal once a day, or ten steps a day, whatever your schedule and your desire calls for. There may be times when you feel like you are going backwards which can be very frustrating. Do not stop! Do not give up! Do not quit! Keep moving forward no matter how hard it may be. As long as you send that one e-mail or make that one phone call that you need to each day, it will take you one step closer to accomplishing your goal.

> How many steps a week can I realistically do?
> How many steps a day can I realistically do?
> What is one thing (or ten) I can do before I go to bed tonight?

Either you run the day, or the day runs you.
~ Jim Rohn ~

It all boils down to using your time productively. You have twenty-four hours in a day. With eight hours of sleep, you have sixteen hours a day, giving you 112 hours in a week to be productive with a healthy sleep cycle. Since you only have sixteen hours a day, stop using it aimlessly; live it with purpose. Time is one thing we can never get back or make more of. No matter how wealthy you are, you do not know when your time bank will abruptly run out. You have the control to run your day by accomplishing the tasks that you want to. The day runs you through traffic, e-mail, phone calls, texts, weather, and anything else that happens in life. Your taking control to run the day can entail listening to audio books while driving; scheduling a time of day for e-mails, phone calls, texting, and social media; and checking the weather the night before. Control your life, or life will control you!

> How can I, or how do I, control "traffic"?

How can I, or how do I, control technology?
What is uncontrollable in my life? How can I control it?
(The answer,"I Can't" is not an answer)

If you do what you've always done, you'll get what you've always gotten.
- Tony Robbins -

This sounds obvious, right? Right! Yet we keep doing the same things and expecting different results. Albert Einstein called that insanity. This applies to relationships, careers, goals, diets…everything! If you ask someone to do something and they do not do it, raising your voice and saying the same thing will not bring different results, you need to reframe the question or statement. If you keep having terrible relationships, you may have to start your next relationship differently; try refraining from sex for a few years to build a solid base—the divorce rate proves the American society is "insanely stupid" in this area. If you are always broke, maybe you need to invest your money instead of buying a pair of shoes you will not wear next year. The top three things people worry about most are their finances, health, and relationships. To improve them, start doing things differently. It's that simple!

How can I start treating my relationships differently?
How can I start treating my health differently?
How can I start treating my finances differently?
(Those still in school, develop good habits now!)

Opportunities don't happen, you create them.
- Chris Grosser -

People whom you consider lucky are not lucky; they worked hard, and took advantage of every opportunity presented to them to produce their own luck. You too can create your own luck by creating your own opportunities. Keep your goals in the front of your mind all day, every day; you will see opportunities you have never seen before. There may be someone you have seen hundreds of times over the years, even someone you do not know, yet that person could be one of your greatest opportunities. To make that person into an opportunity, you must talk to them, and know what you want! Creating opportunities is easy; all it takes is courage to do what others will not. It means doing affirmations every morning and every night before bed. An affirmation is a short, positive, present tense statement of your goal. Doing this will keep your dreams in your mind all day, reminding you to create new opportunities that were always there, but you had not noticed.

What opportunities have I created in the past?
What opportunities have I passed up because I did not have the courage?
Besides affirmations, how am I going to create my next opportunity?

If opportunity doesn't knock, build a door.
- Milton Berle -

Every time you wake up, you wake up to opportunity. What is that opportunity? It is you; your thoughts, your passions, your dreams. You create all the circumstances in your life, which means you were the one who created all the opportunities that came your way. Make it your business to know the right people, make it your job to obtain the right skills, network in the right groups, do your research, get out of your comfort zone. Getting out of your comfort zone is the only way to create opportunities for yourself. If other people do not give you the opportunity, create your own opportunities by meeting the right people who will give you the time to manifest your desires. Other people have their own hopes and dreams they are pursuing. To make yours a reality, you will have to create your own opportunities with hard work, action, and persistence.

> What three opportunities do I need to make me happier?
> Who can give me those opportunities?
> What is their company, position, name, and/or job title?
> How can I make those opportunities happen?
> What steps do I need to take?

Build your own dreams, or someone else will hire you to build theirs.
- Farrah Gray -

The difference between the super successful and the average person is that the super successful make their dreams reality, and the average person works for them. This does not mean every employee or small business owner is average; they could very well be living their dream. The top 1 percent of people considered to be the richest in the world are told by the media that they need to pay their fair share. Is it really fair for someone to work as hard as they did to achieve their dreams, employ thousands, only to pay the average person not to work or try as hard as they did? When you build your own dreams, it is likely that you will hire people to help you build that dream. Stop helping other people build their dreams, start building yours. Do not worry; there are enough average people to go around to help every go-getter!

> What dream am I building that is not mine?
> What dream of mine can I start building?
> What are my first three steps?
> What can I delegate to others to help build my dream?

Your time is limited, so don't waste it living someone else's life.
- Steve Jobs -

The rest of the statement after the quote is, "Don't be trapped by dogma—which is living with the results of other people's thinking. Don't let the noise of others' opinions drown out your own inner voice. And most important, have the courage to follow your heart and intuition. They somehow already know what you truly want to become. Everything else is secondary."

This quote is from Steve Jobs' commencement address at Stanford in 2005. Look within yourself to find the answers to your life questions. Take twenty minutes each day to meditate for the answers, and you will find them. Your time is precious, treat it as such.

> What results am I living that are from other people's thinking?
> How does my heart want me to live?
> What is my intuition telling me?

What you do speaks so loudly that I cannot hear what you say.
~ Ralph Waldo Emerson ~

Actions speak louder than words. Both your words and your actions affect everyone around you. If you tell someone you will do something, be good to your word and do it. If in the past you have not been good to your word, acknowledge that fact and forgive yourself. Don't beat yourself up or go into seclusion about it. Focus on today, and the actions you do daily. Take the third-person view. What actions do you take that others see? Keep your word and your actions congruent. It is better to say nothing or say "no," than promise to do something and then not do it. Your word and your actions affect everyone around you. It does not matter if you spend all day in bed or go out and volunteer. When you seclude yourself, you affect those you could have met by your absence. In the end, you change the world by your actions, or inaction.

> How can I say "no" when I know I won't follow through?
> How did people react after my actions did not back up my words? (Vice Versa too!)
> How did I view other people who acted in a way contrary to what was said?

Luck is a dividend of sweat. The more you sweat, the luckier you get.
~ Ray Kroc ~

There is no such thing as a lucky person. Luck is purely a state of mind. When two people get into a car accident, the lucky person is grateful to be alive, the unlucky person sees only a totaled car and hospital bills. In a raffle, a lucky person does not care if they lose and is happy for the winner; an unlucky person gets upset, and says the drawing was rigged. You call some people lucky because everything is going well for them. But that luck did not appear out of thin air; they worked hard when everyone else was out living life. While you were wasting your life in front of a TV set, they were working up a sweat creating their luck. Remember: when you are doing nothing, there is always someone out there working harder than you to accomplish what you are putting off.

> What luck have I created from hard work?
> What luck did I receive from doing absolutely nothing?
> What can I do to create my own luck?

The difference between ordinary and extraordinary is that little extra.
~ Jimmy Johnson ~

Take the initiative. Go above and beyond of what is expected of you. Put in a little more effort than everyone else. At work, be the first to arrive and the last to leave. There are many ways of reframing this, but they all mean the same thing. Ordinary is average, and average people don't stand out in your mind. When you receive service that is above and beyond anything you experienced, you will remember it, and look at the person providing that service as extraordinary. You can do this in all areas of life; from school to work, from friends to family, from walking down the street to being a customer. No one wants to be average and ordinary, yet very few people actually make that extra effort to stand out from the rest. In the 21st Century, becoming that extraordinary person is getting easier and easier! Give everything "that little extra."

What have I noticed when people put in that little extra?
Where and how can I start putting in extra effort?
What benefits will I directly receive from going above and beyond?

Successful people do what unsuccessful people are not willing to do. Don't wish it were easier, wish you were better.
~ Jim Rohn ~

Becoming a success requires an investment of time and effort. Successful people driven with passion invest as much as 60 to 110 hours per week in their vision and their plan. The average person without a vision works dispassionately, 40 hours or less per week, putting their efforts into someone else's plan. There is a saying, "I'd rather work 80 hours a week so that I don't have to work 40." For successful people, hard work is a choice and has purpose, and that purpose brings joy. For average people, work is an obligation and hard, something to endure, a drudgery to suffer. Successful people are consumed with what they are passionate about, and work hard on their plan to achieve their goals. Average people have no plan and no goals, give away their passion without aim, and when faced with obstacles, give up. Successful people channel their passion into facing obstacles head on, and overcoming them. Average people do nothing with their ideas. Successful people buy time, average people sell their time. Successful people pursue their ideas and turn them into reality. Who do you want to be?

What am I willing to do that successful people do?
What do I already do that unsuccessful people are not willing to do?
What can I do to be better than the average person?

The question isn't who is going to let me; it's who is going to stop me.
~ Ayn Rand ~

If someone does not allow you to do something, do it anyway! People have a tendency to become roadblocks for other people's goals. When you encounter such human roadblocks, you have several options. You can go above them, meaning go to the people who are superiors of the person who just shot you down. You can go around them, meaning do it anyway, but stay off their radar so they do not block you again. You can go under them, meaning proceed with what you wanted to do with the support and knowledge of those who are below the roadblock in power. You can go right through them, meaning you proceed with what you want to do right in front of them, making sure they know you are doing what they told you not to do. There are many examples in real life of how others went above, around, under, or right through people who were roadblocks. Choose the path that applies to you! Never let anyone stop you from achieving; they are too small minded to know better.

> Who are the people in my life who will try and stop me?
> What will I do next time someone tries to stop me? (Be specific, not metaphorical)
> How can I get past my current roadblocks?

Success is the sum of small efforts, repeated day in and day out.
~ Robert Collier ~

A mason is someone who lays bricks to build walls, buildings, walkways, etc. If a mason laid one brick every day during his whole career, by the end of his career, he would have built a great wall or building. The small effort of laying one brick every day eventually adds up to a great achievement. You can do this, too. Figure out what you want to do, and take one step a day to make it happen. Or you can do one step a week, or even three. Depending upon your desire to change your life, you can go as far as taking twenty steps a day. All the small efforts you put forth will eventually add up to one great success. Add up your pennies, and they will eventually make a dollar.

> How many steps can I realistically do every week? Every day?
> What time do I have available during the week to take these steps?
> What time do I have during the weekend?
> What can I sacrifice to free up time to accomplish more?

The most difficult thing is the decision to act, the rest is merely tenacity.
~ Amelia Earhart ~

Think back to when you were in school and had homework to do. The hardest part about homework was starting. The decision to start is the hardest thing to do in all areas of life. Once you start, you will build momentum within yourself to keep going. To build that momentum, you have to be strong and continue for a long time. Your determination to see it to the end will get stronger, and you will not be easily pulled off your task. Tenacity is only important after you first act!

> What experience have I encountered where I was tenacious and succeeded?
> What is the hardest thing for me to start right now?
> How will I and my environment benefit from the completion of what I am "waiting" to start?

Happiness is not something ready-made. It comes from your own actions.
- Dalai Lama -

Happiness in life is not guaranteed; you have to make the appropriate choices that are relevant to you and your dreams in order to be happy. Your happiness in life comes from your thoughts and actions, not one or the other. Since happiness is a state of mind, a choice, it is all in your head. Your actions come from your thoughts which prompted your action. You cannot sit around waiting for happiness to come to you; go out and make things happen which will make you happy. Happiness is not a destination you should hope for; happiness is a part of the journey you take to get to the destination where you want to be. Happiness comes from doing, so do something that makes you happy and you will be happy.

What am I currently doing to make myself happy?
What thoughts make me happy?
What actions can I do to make myself happy and spread happiness to others?

Never leave that till tomorrow which you can do today.
- Benjamin Franklin -

Yesterday is always in the past, tomorrow will never come; the only time you have is today, right now. Now is where the power is. When you have time to do something now, do not talk yourself into doing it tomorrow because chances are you will not do it. You will push it off for tomorrow time and time again. There is no time like the present because that is the only time you live in. The present, today, the immediate now, is all you have. You will have to go through with it at some point if you want to succeed. Going through the actions necessary to succeed only exist today, in the now, your immediate present. They do not exist in your tomorrows and yesterdays; yesterdays no longer matter. The NOW is the only thing that counts!

What have I been putting off for the "tomorrows" which never came?
What have I accomplished in the present that I never did "tomorrow"?
How can I get myself to start doing things today?

Only put off until tomorrow what you are willing to die having left undone.
- Pablo Picasso -

As sad as it is, your life could end before you go to bed tonight. You might not wake up tomorrow. Tomorrow is full of uncertainty; you never know what day will be your last. The only time you have is now, today. Do what is important to you and leave the meaningless tasks for tomorrow. Plan out your days with tasks that mean something to you, something that will help change the lives of others. There is only so much time in a day and you spend eight hours of it sleeping. Every day you have sixteen hours to get the most important tasks of your life done. Every day, every second, is more important than the last because it could all be taken away at any second. Do what you need to do today; do not push it off for tomorrow. You may never get the chance.

What do I keep putting off that is more important than watching tv, video games, social media, etc.?
What do I need to do today?
If I die tomorrow, what will I regret never having done?

Most of the important things in the world have been accomplished by people who have kept on trying when there seemed to be no hope at all.
- Dale Carnegie -
The secret to life is to keep going, keep trying. If your car breaks down on a road trip in the middle of nowhere, some may think there is no hope, and give up because they have not seen a car in hours. Do not give up on your life. Do not give up on your dreams. Do not give up on what is important to you. The great thing about life is that we are all different, which means we all have different ideas of what is important to us. The only way to fail is to give up and quit. Do not quit on what is important to you, that's a wicked habit to create. If it is important enough for you to try once, then it is important enough for you to finish so the rest of the world can benefit.

What is important to me that I gave up on?
How bad do I want what I gave up on?
What is important for me to accomplish now? Why?

Whenever you see a successful person, you only see the public glories, never the private sacrifices to reach them.
- Vaibhav Shah -
Sacrifice is a daily occurrence you may have never noticed before. When you go to school or work, you sacrifice hours you could be outside in the sun with your family and friends. When you play video games, you sacrifice reading a book, doing homework, or improving your life. When you go out with friends on the weekend, you sacrifice time to study or further your career. The public only sees the success a person creates. Successful people make sacrifices that average people think are impossible and inhumane. Entrepreneurs may sacrifice comfort by living in their office or car; valedictorians may sacrifice their weekends to study and do homework; career-oriented people may sacrifice family and friends to make it to the top; police officers and soldiers may sacrifice their lives to protect the greater good. Be conscientious of your decisions and what you are sacrificing.

What result producing activities do I need to do?
What are my biggest time wasters which take me away from successful actions?
What should I sacrifice?
How I can enforce my boundaries with sacrificing to focus on successful actions?

A successful man is one who can lay a firm foundation with the bricks that others throw at him.
- Sidney Greenberg -

Life will give you all sorts of obstacles that might prevent you from accomplishing your goal. Those who are successful take what life throws at them and build upon it. All your life experiences developed you into who you are today. With every situation and circumstance, you have millions of options to choose from. Choose to take what life throws at you and build a firm foundation of integrity, values, loyalty, honesty, responsibility, morality, ethics, and more. It is up to you to decide what to do, and how to respond to all the negativity you will encounter along your way to the top. Turn the negativity life hands you into something wonderful. You choose your own destiny every second. To manifest that destiny you desire, you must do the right thing every chance you get. Use the negativity to help you grow!

> What bricks make up my foundation?
> What negative situation can I look at as a positive for building a firmer foundation?
> What obstacle am I facing right now which will help me grow into a better person?

Success is a function of persistence and doggedness and the willingness to work hard for twenty-two minutes to make sense of something that most people would give up on after thirty seconds.
- Malcolm Gladwell -

Success is your connection to goodwill, endurance, and self-will in order to labor intensely far longer than most people. Hypothetically speaking, if it only took twenty-two minutes to achieve the dreams you desire, the majority of people will give up within thirty seconds. By possessing a steadfast determination towards your end result, you will have the willingness to maintain directed focus creating an outcome of results. The average person can be given a step-by-step guide on how to achieve their desires and they would not even take "thirty seconds" worth of action on it. To become a success with whatever it is you are pursuing, make peace with the fact that it may take years longer than you expect. Hard work pays off in time, willingly put your "twenty-two minutes" of effort into your purpose while maintaining your course of action.

> What challenges have I overcome with persistence?
> What did I learn from those experiences?
> What challenges do I expect to encounter in the near future?
> How will I overcome them?
> What is one thing I will put steadfast persistence towards which the average person would give up on after barely trying?

I have not failed. I've just found ten thousand ways that won't work.
- Thomas A. Edison -

New and great ideas are a common occurrence. You have many great ideas each day. The possibility that the majority of people will make even one attempt to realize one of their millions of ideas is zero percent. Most people put zero effort into attempts at fulfilling their dreams. Most people do not try even once! To try and fail ten thousand times alone is success. Even if Thomas Edison had not invented the light bulb, he was a success for not just trying once, but persisting ten thousand times, learning from it, and trying again. You will never succeed until you try. How badly do you want it? How strong is your desire? Pursue what you are passionate about; then you will try a hundred thousand times until you succeed. When you fail, smile and know you succeeded in identifying one way that didn't work. Get up and do it again differently.

> What motivated me to keep trying until I succeeded?
> What do I want to try again that I had given up on?
> What have I not tried yet which I keep thinking about?

I didn't fail the test. I just found a hundred ways to do it wrong.
- Benjamin Franklin -

In the real world, every day, life is your test. If you fail the first time, you can keep trying until you get it right. There is no set number as to how many times you can try and fail at something until you succeed. When you try to do something and fail, pay attention to the feedback you get so you can do it differently next time, and the next, and the next. As long as you keep trying and applying the knowledge you get from the feedback, you will succeed; you will pass the test of life. Once you leave school, a whole new set of rules applies. You pass in the real world by trying over and over again, learning all the ways that do not work so you can find the one thing that does.

> What have I accomplished after failing the first couple times?
> What did I fail and give up at which I should try again?
> How will I and my environment benefit from it?

It's not whether you get knocked down, it's whether you get up.
- Vince Lombardi -

You will get knocked down, guaranteed. The only time you will not is when you do not try, or do not go after something worth going after. Getting knocked down in life is when you fail at your first attempt, or even your thousandth attempt. What defines you as a winner or a loser is what you do after you do not succeed. Instead of blaming others, complaining about everything that went wrong, or making excuses for your lack of preparation, get back out there and do it again with a new perspective on how to accomplish it. Getting knocked down, failing, is a gift. Failure is the best learning process life can give you. Get back up and go do it again!

> What should I try again?
> What did I learn from my first attempt?
> How am I going to do it differently?
> How will I benefit from trying again?

Fall seven times and stand up eight.
- Japanese Proverb -

Success is always one more try away. If you keep getting knocked down, get back up every time. If you fall seven times and get up seven times, you will get knocked down again. If you get up once more, there is a chance that the eighth time is when your success will come. Life will knock you down, and you will fall on your own; these are givens. You need to get back up and try again. The view at the top is far better than the view from the bottom. Think of the skyscrapers in New York City. From the ground, you are surrounded and feel small. When you get up to the hundredth floor or so, the view is spectacular, and feels like you are on top of the world. Keep getting back up, and the view will get better with each try!

> What did I give up on after numerous attempts?
> What did I accomplish after numerous attempts?
> What "view" do I want for my life?

If you're going through hell, keep going.
- Winston Churchill -

If you end up in a horrible situation, do you just sit there? No! Smart people, winners, will do what they can to get out of that situation; they keep moving forward. Everyone in life has been through hell, but few end up becoming a success. The ones who achieve success do so because they kept moving and doing what they believed to be right. Whenever we are put in a situation we do not want to be in, something we hate, it is in our nature to do what we can to get out of it and come out on whatever side we can. Then there are some people who will accept that they cannot get any better, or believe they do not deserve anything better. They end up living a life of hell every day, because they did not keep going. When you drive in a tunnel, eventually you will come out the other side if you keep moving in the right direction.

> What "hell" have I accepted in life?
> How is accepting this "hell" better than moving forward?
> What do I need to do to get out of that "hell"?

BOOK TWO

The only way to do great work is to love what you do.
~ Steve Jobs ~

Steve Jobs goes on to say "if you haven't found it yet, keep looking. Don't settle. As with all matters of the heart, you'll know when you find it. And, like any great relationship, it just gets better and better as the years roll on. So keep looking until you find it. Don't settle." Great work starts with passion. If you hate what you do, anyone with a love for it will always do a better job. Find what you love to do and go out and do it, do not settle for anything less. You only live once, do not waste it doing the things that make you unhappy. Do not waste your time doing things sub-par where it is just good enough to not get fired. Look within yourself and you will know when you find what you love to do and what you have to do to make it into a reality. Do not settle.

What do I love to do?
How can I make money doing that?
What are my next action steps which I need to take to live a life I love?

I would rather die of passion than of boredom.
~ Vincent van Gogh ~

People who do death-defying stunts do so because that is their passion. It may be to entertain, look death in the eyes, feel the adrenalin rush, push the limits, etc. For whatever reason they do what they do, it is because of their passion. If a doctor would tell them they can no longer skydive or tightrope walk, they would either go out and do it again or become bored and unfulfilled. This is an extreme example but it applies to everyone no matter what your passion is. Once you find your passion, nothing can take its place. It will consume your thoughts and your life. If that love is taken away from you, you become restless. Live your passion or be bored forever!

How did I react when I was not able to do what I love?
What passion do I have which will not leave my thoughts?
What do I do when I am bored?
What can I do differently?

You can do anything, but not everything.
~ Anonymous ~

You have the potential to do anything and be anything you want. However, there is not enough time in the day to be able to do everything. When you put your attention to one thing, you are investing your time and attention to what you want to do. No person has ever been in two places at once. When you try to do everything, in the end you will accomplish nothing. If you do end up accomplishing something, it will be sub par and not the greatest result. Studies show that multi-tasking is not a good skill to have. Your efforts will be displaced in too many other areas. Focus on your core genius to achieve greatness. Your core genius is something you do very well and love to do. Focus on your core genius and delegate everything else that revolves around accomplishing your desired results.

What is everything I can do? (Talent, Skills, Abilities, etc.)
What is the one thing that would make me the happiest achieving?
What are things I do which I am not that good at, which I could easily delegate to someone else?

Take up one idea! Make that one idea your life - think of it, dream of it, live on that idea. Let the brain, muscles, nerves, every part of your body, be full of that idea, and just leave every other idea alone. This is the way to success.
- Swami Vivekananda -

You cannot do everything you want, but you can do anything you want. This is extremely overwhelming for those who have a lot of ideas and talents to take their life in every direction. There is only so much time in a day and so many days in your life. You can pursue everything you want and be almost mediocre at it, or choose one thing and be outrageously successful in all aspects of that niche. With that one idea you choose to pursue, let it consume your thoughts, visions, dreams and actions. When you put aside all the other ideas, it frees up your mind and your time to pursue what truly matters to you and who you want to become; who you want to be known as. Stop multi-tasking and focus!

What is everything I want to pursue?
What do I want to be remembered for when I am gone?
What is one idea I want to center my life around?

Life is not about finding yourself. Life is about creating yourself.
- Lolly Daskal -

Some may say that you must find yourself in order to create yourself. Successful people say that you should discover yourself in order to create yourself. Teenagers are on the hunt for who they are and what they should pursue for the rest of their life. Many middle-aged people talk about finding their passion and making it happen. Create the life you know will make you happy, there is nothing stopping you but you. Through our parents, friends, family, and teachers, we are trained to make safe choices so that we can live that safe life other people expect. We are trained to go to school, work hard, and get good grades in hopes we get into a good college and a good career. Once we have that career, we are told what to do, how much we are worth, when and for how long vacations are, and then we can lose that job at any time our boss choses. Create yourself and do not conform to what other people want you to do.

What is the life I want to create for myself?
What do I need to specifically do to create that life?
What do I believe I can create?

An unexamined life is not worth living.
~ Socrates ~

If you do not examine your life, then you are not growing. When you think about your past, learn from it and grow to give your life meaning. The only way to find the true meaning of life is to look within yourself. There is no right answer, we all have different meanings. Live a life of happiness, self attainment and by accomplishing goals. Through the act of achieving something, with effort, it will make you happy. 100% guaranteed! Live your life with inner happiness and purpose to gain value in all the waking seconds of your life. Make the conscious decision and effort to reach self-actualization and you will live a happy life.

How do I want to look back on the decision I might face right now?
(Be as specific as possible)
What is the greatest accomplishment I can dream of?
(Take more time before you answer)
What are the next 5 goals I will accomplish?

The two most important days in your life are the day you are born and the day you find out why.
~ Mark Twain ~

Our birthdays are very important days, whether you celebrate them or not. In the matter of finding out why we are here, that comes to us at all different ages and in different forms. No two people are alike. Once we do find our purpose in life, that is the day we are "reborn." From there we can commit to fulfilling our purpose, to actually live life the way it was meant to be lived. As time goes on and we have new experiences, our purpose will evolve with us. The key is discover what your purpose in life is right now and start pursuing it. By doing so, you will have new experiences which will point you in different directions to change you and your purpose.

What gives me the most satisfaction?
How can I be of value to others?
What do I believe my personal purpose statement is at this time?
(35 words or less)

The meaning of life is to find your gift. The purpose of life is to give it away.
~ Anonymous ~

Share your talents and ideas with the world. Do not close yourself off from everyone and live a life of solitude, be the change this world is waiting for. If you are a magician or musician, your gift is entertainment. If you can sell toothpicks to a veterinarian, your gift is sales and communication. We all have gifts and talents. Most of them you have not experienced yet so you do not know you have that as a gift. If you are not presented with a situation, how will you ever know you are good at it? Once you find your gift, share it, live it, love it. Figure out a way to make a living doing it. There is a job somewhere and if you can not find that job, create the job. Millions of people create their own jobs, you can too.

> What are my gifts?
> What do I want my gifts to be?
> How can I share them with the world?

Success is...knowing your purpose in life, growing to reach your maximum potential, and sowing seeds that benefit others.
~ John C. Maxwell ~

Success is the journey you take in life, not the destination you are hoping to reach. No two people will take the same journey; they may be similar, but never exactly the same. The destinations are different in numerous ways even when they appear similar. Know what you are searching for and believe in your potential to reach what you find. If you do not help others along the way, your journey will be lonely and you will not be completely fulfilled. Success is not what you gain, but rather, what you do for others. Share your wisdom, talents, tricks, ideas, and whatever else you can give away. Our world is so competitive that people think they must keep everything to themselves to try and make it to the top. That is a mistake. The top is reached by giving your experience away sparingly.

> How am I improving other people's lives?
> How am I living my life's purpose?
> How will I know when I reached my maximum potential?
> What can I do to begin growing?

You must expect great things of yourself before you can do them.
~ Michael Jordan ~

If you do not believe you will do something great, the chances of you doing anything good will drastically decrease. The reason this happens is because if you do not believe you can do something, the chances of you pursuing it are near zero. If you get forced into it, you will not give it everything you've got because you are already expecting to fail, so why try? To be able to complete anything with pride, knowing that you can do it is the beginning point! You have to start somewhere, and that somewhere is knowing that you, and everyone else, can achieve great things as long as you believe in yourself.

> What great things do I expect of myself?
> What great things do I expect to do?
> What great things would I like to believe I can do?

People who are crazy enough to think they can change the world, are the ones who do.
~ Steve Jobs ~

People who call you crazy are what is termed as a "dream stealer" or "small thinker." These people easily give up and they want you to give up too. You can see this everywhere. If anyone calls your dream "crazy," you are onto something big, so hold onto it and pursue it with all your might. Once you come to the conclusion that you can change the world, all the small thinkers and dream stealers will crawl out of the woodwork to let you know their negative limiting opinion. And then when they see you achieving the impossible, they will turn around and support you as if they always did. Think about all the crazies who changed the world: Thomas Edison; Bill Gates; The Wright Brothers; Steve Jobs; Henry Ford; the list goes on for hundreds of pages. They were crazy enough to not listen to all the negative people around them. If they can do it, you can too!

What "crazy" idea did I once have that a small thinker stole from me?
How can I overcome my next dream stealer? (Be specific)
List all my "crazy" world changing ideas.
Which one strikes me as the one I want to pursue?

If you hear a voice within you say "you cannot paint," then by all means paint and that voice will be silenced.
- Vincent Van Gogh -

Practice makes perfect! You can learn any skill you want, from painting to speaking to leading to socializing. Everything that people do was learned at some point in their life. People who are called natural leaders were taught how to be leaders. They have been doing it for so long or had support so there is no voice in their head telling them they cannot lead. You can do whatever you want, even if you think you cannot. If you want to do something but think you cannot, that is when you should do it. When you have a fear of doing something, the more you do it, the less you will experience that fear. Fear is simply a state of mind which you can overcome through repetition.

What is my voice telling me I cannot do?
What was my "practice makes perfect" experience like?
What limiting belief did I have about myself which I do not have now?

Nothing is impossible, the word itself says, "I'm possible!"
- Audrey Hepburn -

The Earth is an astonishing place. It took millions of years for a fire ball in space to turn into a rock. Millions of more years to form water and oxygen. Millions of more years to form plant life. Millions of more years to have living creatures, both in the sea and on land. Dinosaurs came and lived for millions of years and an asteroid took them out, and for millions of years the Earth went through ice ages. If you picture a map and draw a line from L.A. to New York City and considered it a time line of the earth, the dinosaurs lived from L.A. past Ohio. People have only been on this earth for a couple New York City blocks. We are a young species on an "old" planet. The world has recycled itself over time and again. The species and life forms on Earth have not all been found. It seems like every week people uncover something new about this planet we never new before. The Earth and universe prove that absolutely anything is possible! Apollo 11 was the first rocket ship to land on the moon in 1969. Fifty years later our cell phones have more computing power than that spacecraft. Impossible is a word that is left only for people who do not even want to try, they're the losers who will hold you back from winning.

> What did I believe was impossible only to find that it was more than possible?
> What is impossible which I can make possible?
> How can I make the impossible possible?

You can't connect the dots looking forward; you can only connect them looking backwards. So you have to trust that the dots will somehow connect in your future. You have to trust in something - your gut, destiny, life, karma, whatever. This approach has never let me down, and it has made all the difference in my life.
- Steve Jobs -

Whichever direction you take in life, it will leave a footprint of where you have been. When you were a child, you may have had a workbook where you would connect the dots in numeric order. They could have been scattered all over the page or could have been in order. After you connected them, chances are that you created an image to show what you made. Think back to all of the decisions you made and what footprint you left behind. When you remember each one, the dots will all connect into what your life is today. When you look into the future, you do not know what decisions you will have to make and what footprint you will leave behind. You may leave dots all over the page or you may put them in an easy order. In the end, you will have created the life your choices and actions create.

> What do I trust in? (gut, destiny, life, karma, etc.) Explain why!
> Connecting the dots of my past, what life has my decisions created?
> What can I change?
> What approach do I use, or should I use, to trust everything will work out?

To live a creative life, we must lose our fear of being wrong.
- Anonymous -

Everyone has a fear of something—even the most fearless person you can think of. Superman has a fear of kryptonite which he had to overcome to make him strong enough to be Superman. Do not fear fear, confront it head on. Being wrong or politically incorrect is a strong legitimate fear which limits a lot of people from speaking out. When you say something wrong, it opens up a lot of doors to ridicule from those around. Since we choose to make this fear so real, it limits people from speaking out even when they do know the answer. Actions are the same way too. When you do something creative, it is out of the ordinary and considered wrong, you will receive ridicule. A lot of creativity is being suppressed and avoided because of the fear that it will be considered wrong. Stop worrying what other people think. Other people are the ones who will let you know you are wrong. They are wrong for not believing in your creativity. Be creative and achieve success once you leave them behind.

What are my fears?
What is the worst possible thing that can happen when I am wrong?
What am I creative in?

I have learned over the years that when one's mind is made up, this diminishes fear; knowing what must be done does away with fear.
- Rosa Parks -
Fear is always present in everyone's life, even when you know what has to be done. Once you know what has to be done and make up your mind to do it, that fear will diminish to near nothingness. Fear is something that will always be there trying to stop you from doing what you know is right. Make up your mind, commit yourself and the fear will slowly go away only to be replaced by a confident belief in yourself. When you face your fears, you become a stronger individual on the inside and it makes you realize what it is you are truly capable of. Do not let fear stop you. Set a goal, believe you can do it, make up your mind, commit yourself, face your fears and you will overcome everything that stops the average person you'll never hear about. Fear is a state of mind that goes away with action. You know what you need to do, make up your mind and commit to it!

What did I accomplish after I made up my mind to do it?
What fears did I confront after knowing what must be done?
How did I grow as an individual by confronting my fears?

Without leaps of imagination, or dreaming, we lose the excitement of possibilities. Dreaming, after all, is a form of planning.
- Gloria Steinem -
You must never lose your sense of excitement in life. Dreaming helps you plan a fulfilled life. All ideas come from dreaming, using your imagination. Everything begins with a thought. You think about going to a ball game before you actually go. That is the first step in the planning process, thinking. Use your imagination and dream big about all the exciting things that life can, and will, bring you. Keep dreaming in the planning process to make it into reality. Even if you do not go to that "ball game," it is exciting to dream about. Science has proven that when we use our imaginations, the same neurons in the brain light up in an MRI which are used when we actually go through the motions. Your imagination is as real as you and me. It is exciting to day dream and use your imagination to picture all the possibilities life has to offer. Become that day-dreamer you once were but was stolen away from you!

What do I day dream about most often?
What am I dreaming about doing next in life?
What are three possible ways I can imagine to make my dream a reality?

Go confidently in the direction of your dreams. Live the life you have imagined.
- Henry David Thoreau -

"I learned this, at least, by my experiment," Thoreau added. "That if one advances confidently in the direction of his dreams, and endeavors to live the life which he has imagined, he will meet with a success unexpected in common hours. Go confidently in the direction of your dreams. Live the life you have imagined. In proportion as he simplifies his life, the laws of the universe will appear less complex, and solitude will not be solitude, nor poverty poverty, nor weakness weakness." As long as you try for your dreams, you will come closer than you initially imagined. If you do not try, you will always be as far as you are from your dreams in ten years as you are now. Give your dream a shot, it will be worth the effort.

How will achieving my dream change my life?
What are the perfect results of the outcome I dream of?
What do I want to put all my effort into?

The best way to predict the future is to create it.
- Abraham Lincoln -

The easiest way to create your future is through goal setting. When you determine what you want and start taking action toward it, you predict the future. To hypercharge your future prediction, use visualization. This can be done numerous ways. You can create a dream board, which is where you post pictures that show your goal as already accomplished in places where you will see them every day. You can get these pictures from the Internet, magazines, take them yourself, draw or paint them, or any other way you like. Another way is to write down exactly what it is you are working toward. The key here is to spend five to ten minutes a day, once in the morning and once before bed, visualizing your goals as already complete. Tap into the emotions you will have when your goal is reached. Thought backed by emotion is the express train to success.

What will I accomplish in one year? How?
What will I accomplish in five years? How?
What will I accomplish in 10-25 years? (Write about one or both) How?

Cherish your visions and your dreams as they are the children of your soul, the blueprints of your ultimate accomplishments.
- Napoleon Hill -

A blueprint of accomplishment helps you determine your path, what to do next and how to do it. The visions you have of your future accomplishments and the dreams of your life are as precious as your only child. Treat them as such. Nurture and care for them every way you know how. Keep imagining all the possibilities and dreaming up new ideas to expand on your existing ones. Care for them by actually going out and trying to achieve them by turning them into reality. When you accomplish a dream that was once only in your mind, it sends a powerful signal to your subconscious saying that "if you keep producing ideas, I will keep turning them into reality." Your creativity will keep increasing and the ideas will keep getting bigger and better every time you accomplish one!

What visions, dreams and ideas do I hold close to my heart?
What visions, dreams and ideas have I created into reality?
What visions, dreams and ideas do I truly want to be my reality?

Every child is an artist. The problem is how to remain an artist once he grows up.
~ Pablo Picasso ~

When you grow up, do not lose the creativity you once had when you were a child. Do not take the creativity away from a child, teen or any adult either. Promote creativity and imagination. The imagination and creativity of a child is far greater than that of the majority of adults. Those recognized as creative geniuses are geniuses because they return to using their child-like imagination. They bring to their imagination all the knowledge that they learned, but like children, they allow their imaginations to run wild. That is how to be creative. That is how to be an artist. When we start growing up, our surroundings tell us what is possible and what is not possible. Limits to possibility are opponents to the creative imagination. Believe anything is possible and imagine all the possibilities.

What do I enjoy imagining?
What do I remember imagining who I will be when I grow up?
What creative idea do I have?
What are my first steps to turn it into reality?

**Limitations live only in our minds.
But if we use our imaginations,
our possibilities become limitless.**
~ Jamie Paolinetti ~

Our entire reality lies within our minds. What we perceive to be true is probably not even close. There are filters our conscious mind has in which it makes us perceive things how we were taught to see them through experiences and what the people in our lives tell us. We all have limiting beliefs about ourselves which are false, we can do anything we want to as long as we believe in ourselves. We also all have an imagination! When we use our imagination we can do anything. Use your imagination to overcome obstacles. Use your imagination to determine what you want your life to be like. Use your imagination to visualize your end results. Believe your dreams are extremely possible, because they are.

What do I imagine my life will be like?
What is something I cannot do?
Using my imagination, describe in detail how I will do it!
What are all the possibilities I have in my life?

You take your life in your own hands, and what happens? A terrible thing, no one to blame.
- Erica Jong -

American society is notorious for blaming others. Stella Liebeck in 1992 sued McDonald's because she spilled coffee on herself and received third-degree burns. She bought the coffee, she put the coffee between her legs, and she decided to take the lid off. She spilled the coffee on herself. Coffee is hot, children know that. If coffee is not hot, it is less likely you will drink it. She decided to blame McDonald's and was awarded $2.7 million for her choices and behavior. If she had taken responsibility for her actions, it would have been a huge blow to her ego and the American society wouldn't be so sue happy and screwed up. You are responsible for your life. You make the decisions and face the consequences. Stop acting like Stella Liebeck by blaming others for your choices. Take responsibility for your actions!

How have I placed blame on others for my actions?
What stupid choices have I made that I blamed others for?
What past actions do I need to take responsibility for? How?

Education costs money. But then so does ignorance.
- Sir Claus Moser -

Ignorance: Lack of knowledge, understanding, or education. - Merriam-Webster
Ignorance is not bliss. Ignorance is expensive and time consuming. If you start a project and do not have the appropriate knowledge, you may have to trash all your work and start over again with the new knowledge you could have easily found. It costs time and money to go to school, buy at-home trainings, attend seminars, take workshops, and read books. Ignorance costs you time and money, sometimes a lot more time and money than if you did your homework and knew what you were getting yourself into. A lot of people are all about jumping in with both feet and learning as you go. That is the thing, jump in and then figure out what you need to learn before you spend a lot of time and money on something that will end up in the garbage.

Honestly, how am I ignorant?
How has my knowledge saved me both time and money?
What resources are available for me to gain more knowledge?
(Do not be vague! i.e. google, seminars, workshops, trainings, etc.)

Keep away from people who try to belittle your ambitions. Small people always do that, but the really great make you feel that you, too, can become great.
- Mark Twain -

Small people will always do small things. They are the ones who will be forgotten. Successful people will help you become successful. If they do not at least point you in the right direction, they are not the successful people you want to emulate.

When you tell a small mind a big goal, they will become your dream stealer. By overcoming these terrible personalities, you will achieve greatness and be remembered far longer than a small person. When you meet a successful person who truly believes in you and your "crazy" ideas, that alone will help you become great. The fastest way to become successful is to help other people become successful. The greatest leaders help people become better than they are in every way.

Who have I belittled in the past and what can I do to support them now?
What can I do to help another person become great?
What can I do to meet the really great people so they can help me become great?

It wasn't raining when Noah built the ark.
- Howard Ruff -

It does not matter if you are religious or not. This quote has nothing to do with religion. The background is that God told Noah to build an ark in the middle of the desert where there was no body of water or rain. Look it up if you want to know more (Genesis 5:32 - 10:1). This quote means "hope for the best, prepare for the worst." By preparing for the future, you will be much better off, you may even save your life. By preparing for the worst to happen, you will be more flexible when things do not go your way. Thinking and planning ahead are tremendous success skills we will all use at some point, if we are smart enough to acquire them. You plan your trip to the grocery store, a night out with your friends, when you will exercise, etc. Since you already know how to plan ahead, why not plan ahead for 40 days of global rain while living in a desert?

How much time do I spend thinking about preparing for my future?
What do I need to do to prepare for my future? How will I do this?
How can I prepare for the worst on my next endeavor?

If you can't explain it simply, you don't understand it well enough.
- Albert Einstein -

When you are learning something new, test your knowledge by explaining it to a child under ten years old. You will truly understand something when you can explain it in minimal words so anyone can understand the core concept. When you do not fully understand, it is hard to explain it unless you memorize a short statement designed to do just that. It is your responsibility to know what you are talking about. The Law of Attraction is a great example. People who first hear about it try to explain it to someone else and fail miserably. To explain The Law of Attraction to someone it is best to put it into practice and read the endless books that are out there. Become a practitioner! If you do not understand something well enough to explain it simply, it is your responsibility to either fully understand it or keep silent when others are speaking on the topic.

What are the subjects I can explain simply?
How much effort did it take to gain that knowledge?
What do I want to fully understand?
What conversations to I need to exclude myself from because I do not understand it? (Politics and Religion is an answer for everyone!)

If you want to achieve excellence, you can get there today. As of this second, quit doing less-than-excellent work.
~ Thomas J. Watson ~

Excellence is as simple as doing excellent things in an excellent way. You can start today, right now, by staying away from doing things that are less than excellent. In turn, when you do something, strive to do more than excellent work. Go above and beyond of what is expected of you, regardless of immediate external reward or pay scale, have trust and faith the rewards will come later. To achieve this, do a phenomenal job every chance you get. You get hundreds to thousands of chances every day to project excellence. There are a lot of people counting on you to do outstanding work. Your life of excellence is top priority!

What do I do less than excellent work in?
What could happen if I do excellent work in areas that I am slacking in?
What do I need to do to consider my work as excellent?

Be more concerned with your character than with your reputation. Your character is what you really are while your reputation is merely what others think you are.
~ Dale Carnegie ~

Dr. Daniel Amen observed the 18-40-60 rule. At the age of 18 all you care about is your reputation and what others think of you. At 40 years young, you realize that it does not matter nor do you care what others think of you. At 60 years young, you finally realize that no one was ever thinking of you. They are too busy caught up in their own lives thinking of themselves and how they will survive. You cannot fully control your reputation, but you can control your character. Some synonyms of character are honor, moral, incorruptible, honest, responsible, ethical, approachable, kind, caring, integrity, etc. Be an honest, moral person who does the right thing and you will possess attributes which successful people have.

Why is my character more important than my reputation?
What characteristics do I have?
(List 5 positive and 5 negative!)
What character traits will make me proud to have?

I've learned that people will forget what you said, people will forget what you did, but people will never forget how you made them feel.
~ Maya Angelou ~

People remember things with a strong emotion attached to them, good or bad. They may or may not remember what you said or did, but they will surely remember how you made them feel. Think about the people in your past who made you feel good and then think about those with a negative feeling attached to them. The chances of you remembering exactly what was said or happened is low. On the other hand, the stronger the emotion that is attached to it, the more details you will remember. Memory is also a tricky thing because we remember what we perceive to be true at the time. Also, every time we recall a memory, it is susceptible to manipulation from the environment in which we recall it. Focus on making people feel good; your words and actions will follow suit.

How have I made people feel good in the past?
What can I do to make someone feel good in my immediate present?
What did you just do?
What will be my "go-to" actions or words to make others feel good?

Success is liking yourself, liking what you do, and liking how you do it.
- Maya Angelou -
Happiness is success. Being completely fulfilled with your life is success. Loving how you earn money is success. Putting your best effort into everything you do is success. Having a loving and caring relationship with yourself and those around you is success. When you add all these together you get something spectacular, a successful life. When you are happy with yourself, what you do, and the effort that you put forth, people will see that. You will see that. You must like yourself first before you can like what you do. Do what you love everyday!

What do I like about myself?
What do I like to do?
What do I like about the effort I put forth?

A truly rich man is one whose children run into his arms when his hands are empty.
- Anonymous -
Being rich has nothing to do with your bank account. In the end, on your death bed, it is the people you love and who love you that matter. To love and be loved is what makes you rich. True love is something money will never be able to buy. You can try to buy "love" until your bank account runs dry or you cut them off; but there was never any love to begin with. In this world, even in your own community, there are many families who do not talk to each other. Parents that no longer talk to their children because of some disagreement. If this is you, stop being stubborn, swallow your pride, and give your child, parent, sibling, or friend a call before you even read past the end of this paragraph. Life without love is not a life worth living. If you do not have children or your parents have passed away, there still are people who care about and love you. Embrace them with open arms!

What can I do to show my family I love them? (without spending one cent)

How did the love of someone else positively effect me?
How can I show my love to the other people in my life?

Knowledge is being aware of what you can do. Wisdom is knowing when not to do it.

- Anonymous -

Many people lack the knowledge of knowing what they are capable of. Many think that they are capable of tasks that they are unprepared for or will never be able to do better than others. Knowing when to act is where your wisdom shines. You can have all the knowledge in the world, know everything about everything, and still achieve nothing. That is why knowledge is not power! It is only when you have the wisdom to know when to use your knowledge, then you must act on it. You probably can remember a time when you knew what to do and how to do it but failed to act. You had the wisdom of knowing but still failed the most important part, acting on your wisdom. Then there are times when you should not have done anything but you did not possess the wisdom to refrain you from acting. Having only good intentions to do something is the same thing as not doing anything. Acting on your wisdom will define who you are and what you accomplish.

What happened when I acted against my wisdom?
What happened when I acted on my wisdom?
How can I start implementing my knowledge when necessary?

Blessed are those who can give without remembering and take without forgetting.

- Anonymous -

It is important to give back to the community through volunteering and doing good deeds for other people; it is not important to remember these moments. When someone does something good for you, never forget it. Think in terms of doing favors for each other. When you do someone a favor, forget about it. Them returning the favor is not that important, do not expect it to happen. When someone does you a favor, do not forget about it. Make sure you pay them back tenfold. Stop thinking, "me, me, me" and start thinking in terms of helping other people without expecting anything in return. When you expect someone to return the favor and they fail to do so, you become bitter towards that person, and in turn, you suffer. The thoughts you have for others project onto you. Do yourself a favor and forget about what you do for others and return the favor for those who have helped you.

Who did a favor for me that I did not return yet?
What will I do for them?
What favor did I do for someone that made their life easier?
What can I do for other people and not expect anything in return?

If you cannot do great things, do small things in a great way.
- Napoleon Hill -

A lot of little things make up the great things. When you are doing the small, seemingly meaningless tasks, do them in a way that displays greatness. Even when you are the most successful person in the world, your present, the now, will always consist of doing small things. It is in these small things that make up your life, they add up to greatness. How you handle yourself, act, and think during your small tasks will end up defining who you are and limiting yourself when you do the bigger tasks. By creating the habit of doing your best every chance you get, you will live the best life you can imagine. It all depends on how you approach and tackle all the small tasks that will determine how great or not so great your present will be.

What great thing are all the small things in my life adding up to?
What were the results after I did a great job on a small thing?
How can I remind myself to develop the habit of constant greatness?

The real opportunity for success lies within the person and not in the job.
- Zig Ziglar -

Most people have to start at the bottom of the company to work their way up. Every job, every task, is just as important as the next in order for a company to work properly. To get promoted, you are judged by how you do your job, not by the job you have. To stand above the rest, you must go above and beyond everyone else. When a person works hard and learns as they go, they open up more opportunities for success than someone who just does what they need to do to not get fired. Show the world your ambition and be presented by all the opportunities you can imagine. Your success lies within you, not within the tasks you are assigned. The successful person sees a necessary task and the average joe looks at it as a meaningless task. Your perception of what you do defines who you are and who you will become. Keep your head up and look at everything as worthwhile!

What "meaningless" tasks have I been assigned?
How can I be great with it?
How can I view my "meaningless" tasks so they are more important?
What opportunities will open up to me by taking the initiative?

Life is not measured by the number of breaths we take, but by the moments that take our breath away.
- Maya Angelou -

You can either measure your life by how long you live, or by all the experiences that you have lived through. A moment that takes your breath away will be a moment you will remember for the rest of your life. As humans, the memories we have of the past is what makes us into who we are. The moments which take our breath away are the moments worth remembering. These are the moments which make us happy to remember and they are the ones we hope to never forget. Pay closer attention to life so you do not miss those moments that could take your breath away. Start showing up to places when you do not feel like it, talk to strangers, face your fears, go out of your comfort zone; anything that will put you into a position to experience a happy moment in which it could take your breath away.

What are my happiest memories?
What was the last moment which took my breath away?
What can I specifically do to put myself in the position to experience happiness?

Don't raise your voice, improve your argument.
- Anonymous -

Communication is one of the most important life skills. Simply getting louder does not persuade. To win many arguments and negotiations, you have to start with communicating properly. It only takes one person to initiate this process. Get to know people and make your arguments relatable to them. Be empathetic. Understand how they feel and voice your agreement. Tell them how you felt at one time that relates back to what the argument is about. Finish with telling them what you figured out from it all and what you have now. There are many more ways to win arguments and negotiations. Find ways that work for you. Study NLP! Getting louder only to repeat yourself is ineffective and annoying. Step up your communication skills!

What do I normally argue about? With whom?
How can I effectively communicate to avoid arguments?
What questions should I ask to effectively communicate?

It is better to fail in originality than to succeed in imitation.
- Herman Melville -

Reinvent the wheel if you believe you need to. In some situations it will be easier and necessary to use what other people have already created. Stay true to yourself and be original. You are your most important asset, do not falter to what other people do. When you copy others to become successful, your accomplishments will not be as gratifying as when you do it yourself, your way. Network marketing companies are notorious for providing the way to success. Definitely follow their blueprint to success, but be original along the way while making sure to take into consideration all their proven do's and don'ts. Just stay original!

What areas of my life do I need to be more original in?
How can I be more original?
What do I find myself imitating most often?

Do not worry if you have built your castles in the air. They are where they should be. Now put the foundations under them.
- Henry David Thoreau -

Depending upon how you perceive this quote, you can take it a couple different ways. You can think of your "castles in the air" as either your dreams, or look at them as projects you jumped into with both feet before doing all your research. You may even see this as something completely different. Either way, you are exactly where you should be in life at every turn. With your dreams, put the foundation underneath with action. When it comes to projects, research what you need to. In every instance you can fathom, ask people who have already done it. Successful people love answering questions on how they became that way.

What dreams do I need to start building foundations under? How?
What do I need to do more research in to make an educated decision?
Who are 5 people I can ask for advice?
(HINT: Do not need to know them personally!)

You can't use up creativity. The more you use, the more you have.
- Maya Angelou -

This quote is missing the rest of what she said which is vitally important. "It is our shame and our loss when we discourage people from being creative. We set apart those people who should not be set apart, people whom we assume don't have a so-called artistic temperament, and that is stupid....Too often creativity is smothered rather than nurtured. There has to be a climate in which new ways of thinking, perceiving, questioning are encouraged. People also have to feel they are needed." When you use your creative imagination, you will become even more creative. This world is in desperate need of creative people who are not afraid of the small-minded individuals who are stuck in archaic ways of thinking and doing things. Your creativity will never diminish regardless of how many times you use it. Creativity only gets better and stronger.

What creative ideas do I have?
What creative ideas have I made into reality?
How can I use my creative imagination more often?

Nothing in the world is more common than unsuccessful people with talent.
- Anonymous -

You can be an extremely talented artist and work as a science teacher. You could be extremely talented with numbers but work as a policeman. These two positions are successful for those whose life it coincides with. Success comes when you are happy, live to your full potential, and impact the greater good by doing what you are most talented at. People with great potential end up taking the safe way out because they talk themselves out of doing it or are too scared to try. You become successful by setting high goals and keep trying until you reach them. It is common that people who have talent do it easier and faster with less effort. Those with less knowledge and talent are the ones who are successful in the public eye because they try and try and try until they succeed. Naturally, talented people tend to think they don't have to work that hard, and in the end, wind up unsuccessful.

What are my talents? (HINT: Ask family and friends!)

What talent makes me happiest when I think about it or use it?
How could I make a living doing that?
What opportunities need to be opened up to me?
How can I make that happen?

Failure is the condiment
that gives success its flavor.
~ Truman Capote ~

Think of success as a hot dog, or if you are vegetarian, as a soy dog. When you put condiments on it like ketchup, mustard, relish and sauerkraut, it makes the hot dog that much better. If you became an instant success with no failures, it will never taste as good because you did not put in the work, it was handed to you on a silver platter by someone else. Success is not about the destination, it is about the journey. The journey is all about failing, learning from those failures, and persevering until you become a better person to reach your successful destination. What you learn and who you become are the most important parts of success, no one can take that away from you. What you learn and who you become will be with you forever, and which you can pass on to others to help them.

Last time I failed, what did I learn?
How has failure been a blessing in disguise? (Come up with 3 reasons!)
How can I look at my past failures as a success?

Success is walking from failure to failure with no loss of enthusiasm.
~ Winston Churchill ~

You will fail way more times than you succeed. One of the greatest players in Major League Baseball history is Hank Aaron. After 23 years in the Major League, Hank Aaron had 755 home runs and struck out 1,383 times. Notice: he struck out almost twice as often as he hit home runs. You can look at that record as a failure or a success story. The Hall of Fame looks at it as a success. Every time he went up to the plate, his enthusiasm was that of a home-run-hitting champion. Keep your head up like Hank Aaron! Know that everyone fails at everything first, before they eventually end up succeeding. Unless you strike out in a stadium full of people, no one will see you fail. People do not remember stories of failure, they remember good things, success stories. For those people who remember other people's failures, they are failures themselves. Hank Aaron's strike-out stats prove success, not failure.

What was my worst "strike out"?
What was my greatest "home run"?
How did I overcome failure in the past only to succeed?

Success does not consist in never making mistakes, but in never making the
same one a second time.
~ George Bernard Shaw ~

Making a mistake is inevitable for everyone in life. We all make mistakes, and if you deny it then you think way too highly of yourself. When you make a mistake, learn from it and how to prevent yourself from making the same mistake again. When the situation arises again, do it differently. You may make another mistake again but at least it is not the same mistake as last time. Learn from the feedback that you receive and do it again differently. If you keep making different mistakes and correcting yourself every time, as long as you keep trying, eventually you will produce the outcome you desire.

What mistakes do I continuously make?
What can I do differently next time?
How would I like to see myself ideally react to it?

You may only succeed if you desire succeeding; you may only fail if you do not mind failing.
~ Philippos ~
You get what you expect and accept in life. If you do not accept failure, you will succeed. If you do not mind failing, you will fail. Over time, you may come to expect failure and stop trying altogether. If you are at that point, you can change it today. Desire is one of the strongest emotions when it comes to being successful. Desire allows you to persevere through all the failures and negativity life has to offer. Failure should never be an option. If life was a war, retreat is an option. Take a step back, gather your thoughts, figure out what you learned, and go back at it.

What are my desires?
What do I desire the most?
What will I gain from succeeding?

By failing to prepare, you are preparing to fail.
~ Benjamin Franklin ~
What makes you think you can succeed if you are not prepared? Sports teams practice and send out scouts to prepare for games. Physicists study physics and gain the knowledge they need so they can obtain a job and excel at it. You will never fail if you try and try again. The only time you fail is if you either give up or do not even try. When you are out not preparing, there will always be someone out there preparing, those are the ones who will succeed after passing you up. If you do not prepare a resume, you will fail at producing one when an employer asks for it. Having more knowledge and using it will help you be more prepared than your competition. You cannot have a successful fundraiser if you do not prepare for it months in advance. Nothing will come easy and success will not come overnight. Prepare for what you are about to do!

How badly did I fail when I did not prepare?
What else can I do to prepare for the next adventure I am pursuing?
What happened when I not only felt prepared, but when I was actually prepared?

To avoid criticism; do nothing, say nothing, be nothing.
- Elbert Hubbard -

Who you are now is all you will ever be if you try to avoid criticism. There are billions of people in this world from all different backgrounds and all sorts of flawed opinions on how you should act. No matter what you do, you will offend others, this is a guarantee. If you are not receiving criticism, you are doing something wrong. The only time when you know you are on track is when some people criticize your dreams, goals, actions, thoughts, etc. No one is "perfect" except for the person doing the criticizing. Getting past these situations is not the easiest, but when you do, it will make you stronger to overcome the next small-minded criticizer.

What have I done to be criticized? What did I do after?
What benefits can I come up with by being, saying and doing nothing?
What benefits can I come up with by being criticized for
being, saying and doing everything I know I can do?

What seems to us as bitter trials are often blessings in disguise.
- Oscar Wilde -

We only live in the present moment, there is nothing else but now. We look back on yesterday and dream about tomorrow. Today is what we live in to experience all the opportunities, successes, and failures of life. As we go through the years, we may have a negative perception of what is happening or what just happened. Sometimes it may take months or decades before you realize that it was actually a blessing for that to happen. When life takes a different direction, you will be presented with all new possibilities which never would have been available before the obstacle, problem, loss, etc. Every bad circumstance will eventually turn into something good, it is a law of the Universe.

What has been my blessing in disguise?
What "bitter trials" am I experiencing currently in my life?
What are all the possibilities these "bitter trials" possess?

If you want to lift yourself up, lift up someone else.
- Booker T. Washington -

To be happy, make someone else happy. Without going into details, the power of the subconscious mind is spectacular. When you help others, you help improve your subconscious. You can help lift others up with a simple smile, holding the door open, letting a car merge into your lane, picking up something someone dropped, and most importantly, volunteering for a nonprofit that is close to your heart. Community service is a great way to give back to everyone that has helped you and a way to help others who are unable to help themselves. When you help others and see the gratitude in their eyes, it is a surefire way to lift yourself up. There are countless of things you can do each day, it is up to you to do what you know is right.

What volunteer opportunities do I have that I have not taken advantage of, yet?
How can I help other people who do not ask for it? (Be Specific)
What have I done before to lift someone up which I can do again?

It's not the years in your life that count. It's the life in your years.
- Edward J. Stieglitz -

Live to 100 or live to 30, doing something worthwhile is the only thing that matters. Some believe it is better to die a young meaningful life than to live to be the oldest person in the world and achieve nothing, except for being the oldest person in the world. It is better to die living your life than it is to live your life dying. In the end, it is what we give back to others that really counts. Life is about the experiences you live through, not the longevity of it. Go out and live your life to the fullest. Do something different, travel to new places, meet new people, face your fears, learn new things; experience everything that life has to offer. To live a meaningful life, be selfishly selfless. When you are selfless to others, it creates happiness in yourself. Be selfish and do selfless acts to make you happy.

How can I leave the world a better place?
What specifically do I need to do to leave the world a better place?
What things do I want to try which will benefit others before I pass away?

I don't want to get to the end of my life and find that I lived just the length of it. I want to have lived the width of it as well.
- Diane Ackerman -

Picture a balance beam in a gymnastics gym. Each end signifies the beginning and end of your life no matter how long you live. You can either spend your whole life on the balance beam or you can use the entire gymnasium and experience a whole lot more. You will gain new skills and strengths which will take you farther in the competition of life. Get off your balance beam and experience the uneven bars, vault, pommel horse, still rings, parallel bars, and the high bar. Do not be scared to experience everything life has to offer. When you come to the end of your life, you will regret not having done more.

What is on my bucket list? (Use a notebook to make a list of 102+ goals)
What do I want to experience this year?
What do I want to achieve?

Few are those who see with their own eyes and feel with their own hearts.
- Albert Einstein -

It is completely natural for people to get manipulated by other people and their opinions. Most of the time, opinions came from someone else which came from someone else and down the line it goes. Other people's opinions, dreams, ideas, passions, etc. are theirs and theirs alone. We as people want everyone to agree with us and take on our own views of the world, and it happens more often than it should. When you see life through your own eyes and feel with your own heart, that essentially means you are your own person and do not let anyone make you think otherwise. You know what is right, so do what is right!

What views of the world do I have that are from other people?
What am I going to do different?
How would I like myself to perceive the world and the situations around me?
What happened when I did not follow what my instincts told me?

If you keep saying things are going to be bad, you have a chance of being a prophet.
- Isaac B. Singer -

Merriam-Webster defines Prophet as, "one who foretells future events". *Wikipedia* defines Expectancy Theory as, "An individual will decide to behave or act in a certain way because they are motivated to select a specific behavior over other behaviors due to what they expect the result of that selected behavior will be." When you expect something bad will happen, you will act accordingly to make it happen. You predict the future every time. Do yourself a favor and start expecting only good things with positive languaging. When you do this, you will see a shift in your results because your behavior will change based upon your thoughts.

How does believing in myself affect my motivation?
(Give a specific example!)
What happened when I expected the worst to happen?
What was my behavior before it happened?
How is expecting the best to happen a healthy mindset?

We become what we think about most of the time, and that's the strangest secret.
- Earl Nightingale -

If you have thoughts of anger and hate, you will project anger and hate on to others. If you have thoughts of love and peace, you will project love and peace. In both cases, whether you think about love or hate, you will become that person. You cannot have thoughts of self-pity all the time and lead a large organization effectively. Great thoughts bring about great actions. Weak thoughts bring about weak actions and weak results. Just like "you are what you eat," you are what you think. Start thinking about thinking. Notice your thoughts, and take control of your thoughts to be positive until it becomes habit.

What do I think about most of the time?
What do I want to become?
What are the thoughts I will need to become that person?

I am an optimist. It does not seem too much use being anything else.
- Winston Churchill -

W. Clement Stone was known for being an inverse paranoid. Being paranoid means that everyone, the world, is out to get you and do you harm. An inverse paranoid is someone who believes that the world is conspiring to bring them only good, success. When you are an optimist, you believe that only good will happen to you instead of worrying about everything that will go wrong. Optimism is the base of The Law of Attraction. What you think about yourself and about others will determine what you see in life, it is what will happen to your life. Expect to live a great successful life and you drastically increase your chances of passing up every average person around you.

What thoughts do I have which are not of an optimistic nature?
What can I do to remind myself to catch my negative thoughts and change them to that of an optimist?
What thoughts consume my mind?
What do I need them to be?

If you look at what you have in life, you'll always have more. If you look at what you don't have in life, you'll never have enough.
- Oprah Winfrey -

Always give thanks for everything you have. Stop thinking about what you do not have. Each morning wake up saying the simple words, "thank you." When you are brushing your teeth say it as well. Keep your mind focused on everything you are grateful for throughout the day. The book and movie, *The Secret*, shared the idea of a gratuity rock: a simple stone that you can find on the ground anywhere. Find a small stone you like. Carry it in your pocket, and every time you touch it, you give thanks for something you have. In the morning you will touch it once to put it in your pocket, and at the end of the day touch it to take it out for the next day. Being grateful just twice a day is two times more often than most. The simple act of being grateful for what you have goes a long way. It will change your life, as it has for millions of others!

What do I have in my life?
What am I grateful for?
Who do I need to call and thank, or send a thank you card/email to?

The most common way people give up their power is by thinking they don't have any.
- Alice Walker -

No matter what has happened to you in the past and what situation you are in now, you are the only one with the power to change it. If you allow someone else to come in and change it for you, you have zero power and control over your life. Everyone in the world is able to control their own life as long as they do not give up their power. There are still things in life you have no power or control over, like events that happen to you. The greatest power—and in fact the only power you ever truly have—is to control your thoughts and your actions. When you control these two, you control your outcomes.

What outcome did I receive when I gave up my power?
What situation am I currently in which I can "flex" my power? How?
What power do I have besides my thoughts and actions?

I know for sure that what we dwell on is who we become.
- Oprah Winfrey -

Thoughts are things. What you think about becomes words. The words you think and say eventually become actions. Your actions eventually make who you are and become. The only way to control your actions is by controlling your thoughts. It is a lot easier said than done. You must think about thinking. Think about the thoughts you have and start controlling them. When you dwell on something, meaning that it consumes your mind, you introduce emotion to your thoughts. Thoughts backed by emotion is the most powerful thing our mind can do. Whether it is positive or negative—whether you want it to be reality or not—what you dwell upon eventually becomes who you are, both inside and out!

Who do I want to become?
What thoughts are dominating my mind?
What thoughts do I need to become the person of my dreams?

A mind is like a parachute, it doesn't work if it isn't open.
- Frank Zappa -

Jumping out of an airplane is an exhilarating experience. The only way you will survive is if your parachute opens. The parachute slows you down, gives you control in the open sky, and helps you land safely in a predetermined destination. Your mind is the same way. When you open your mind to new experiences, learning new skills, and meeting new people, you allow your mind to work the way it was meant to. When you keep an open mind to opportunities that present themselves, you will have more choices to help land at your predetermined destination. Determine where you want to go and by opening your mind to life, you will be able to maneuver your way to where you want to land.

What brain games do I play?
What are my options?
Which ones will I actually play?
What situations am I experiencing in which I need a more open mind?
How did I experience having an open mind?
What happened?

When I hear somebody sigh, 'Life is hard,'
I am always tempted to ask,
'Compared to what?'
- Sydney J. Harris -

It does not matter if you say "life is hard" or "this is hard." What are you comparing it too? Vacuuming is hard when you compare it to laying in bed all day. Swimming a couple laps is hard when you compare it to vacuuming. Life is not hard, life is what you make of it. If you make it hard by comparing it to something extremely easy, then yes, life is hard. The reason why life is easy is because all you have to do is live in the present tense, in the now. You do not have to worry about the past or organize your future, just live in the now by taking the right steps and do what you feel is right every step of the way. If you want to compare life to something, compare it to those lives who lived in Nazi concentration camps, those who were prisoners of war, those who were enslaved. Life is not hard! Get over it!

How did I choose to make my life hard?
What can I compare my life to so that it does not appear to be as hard?
How can I make my life easier? (List 5 examples!)

The elevator to success is out of order. You'll have to use the stairs... one step at a time.
~ Joe Girard ~

There is no get-rich-quick scheme that works. No one will hand you success on a silver platter. No one can do your push-ups for you to make you physically fit. You have to do it yourself, with hard work. When going to the top of a skyscraper, it is a lot easier to take an elevator, where you just stand and wait, than it is for you to climb a hundred stories. To be successful, you must bypass the easy train and go up the hundred flights of stairs, one step at a time. Success is so much sweeter when you work for it yourself. In life, it is not the destination you are working toward, it is the journey. You will learn and grow, and become a better person along the way. If you keep taking the elevator, you will become fat and lazy. Get fit and take those stairs to success. Hard work pays off in time.

What did I notice when I tried to take the easy way out?
What steps do I need to take to succeed?
If I look at it as one step at a time, what are my next ten action steps to take?

The only place where success comes before work is in the dictionary.
~ Vidal Sassoon ~

Work is the displacement of energy to create motion in some way. It takes work to create the life of your dreams. Every day, being successful takes energy—work that you'll love in most instances. You will never be a success at anything sitting in front of the TV, playing video games, reading fiction, and/or doing nothing, unless you believe being a lazy bum is success. The world is more than fair, you get what you deserve every time. If you do not have what you want right now, that is the Universe telling you that you do not deserve it yet. You get back what you put in—nothing more, nothing less!

What areas am I slacking in?
What do I put a lot of work into?
What are my results?
What do I need to receive in order to be satisfied with the results I produce?

I have been impressed with the urgency of doing. Knowing is not enough; we must apply. Being willing is not enough; we must do.
- Leonardo da Vinci -

If you want to get something done, then you must do. The bigger the accomplishment, the bigger the action. Most people get stuck in the mindset of thinking and thinking, but never actually take action. Knowing what to do and how to do it is never enough: you must also apply the knowledge that you have. One possible reason for not taking action is that you see others doing the same thing and are scared to fail while others are succeeding. You may end up being intimidated by the success of others. Knowledge and willingness are never enough to make it a reality. You must apply and do. Always!

How can I start applying my knowledge which I have not used before?
What am I willing to do but have not, yet?
What do I know and am willing to do?
How can I apply my knowledge to do it?

Be purposeful. Be patient, and be active.
- John Assaraf -

Do not wait for success and opportunities to come to you. You must be proactive. Do more than what is expected of you by taking the initiative. In doing so, you will get noticed and opportunities will start presenting themselves. At this point you will be prepared to see and take advantage of every opportunity that comes your way. Know your reasons for doing things; from the overall objective to the purpose of your daily actions. With consistent action, it is only a matter of time before you obtain the results you were working towards. Be patient, it usually takes a few years longer to achieve a big goal than one would have initially hoped for. Be active, you are the only one who has control over the completion of your desires.

What are the opportunities I see in my life pertaining to my goals?
How can I create more opportunities?
What further actions can I do to provide more opportunities?

You may be disappointed if you fail, but you are doomed if you don't try.
- Beverly Sills -

Trying and failing is better than regretting you did not try at all. When it comes to the end of your life, do not have a list of things you never tried because you were to scared to fail. Failure is feedback to help you adjust and calibrate your next attempt. With every try, you are that much closer to accomplishing. Not succeeding at something you tried your best at is very disappointing and can stop a lot of people from trying again. Pat yourself on the back and applaud your efforts because the major majority of people will never try once. Trying does not set you up for disappointment, trying sets you up to become more successful than the average person who does not even think about trying. Keep trying and failing. As long as you don't give up, you will accomplish your goal!

What disappointments have I had to endure?
What will I regret never trying at least once? (List Everything)
What would I like to try again?

Great thoughts speak only to the thoughtful mind, but great actions speak to all mankind.
- Theodore Roosevelt -

If you have an open mind to new experiences, you will be more open to great ideas. Everyone in life gets more than one great idea; what separates greatness from average is action. Actions that are considered to be great end up changing the world. A great idea that took a lot of effort and persistence were the car, light bulb, phone, computer, electricity, etc. Having the idea is one thing, acting on that idea and seeing it through is what will speak to all mankind. In the end, what you do is all that matters. No one will benefit from your great ideas, the world will benefit from your great actions. You may never get famous or be recognized for your actions, but your actions, even one smile, can change someone's world.

What actions from someone else changed my life?
What great idea can I put into action to benefit all of humankind?
What do I need to start acting on?

Do what you can, where you are, with what you have.
- Teddy Roosevelt -

You are the only person who can truly stop you. Once you have the desire to get something done, there is no obstacle too big which you will not be able to conquer. At every chance you get, you need to do whatever it is that you can do no matter where you are. To get anything done, you will have to use the resources available to you. Resources can come in the forms of books, internet, knowledge, people, material things, etc. Get creative to do what you know you can do. Believe in yourself and it will not matter who you are with, where you are, or the obstacles that you are facing. Keep trying and do whatever it is that you think you can do. Doing something is far better than doing nothing. Stop thinking that you are not capable, you will surprise yourself!

What can I do to help someone this week?
Who will it benefit besides me?
What resources are available to me to do what I can?
What other resources do I need?
How can I acquire them?

If not us, who? If not now, when?
- John F. Kennedy -

The best time is now and the best person is you, period! Other people can not do everything. If the people who create and change everything thought that someone else would do it, we would still be living in the stone age without fire or the wheel.

When you get an idea, the best person to make it a reality is you. The best time to do something is now. Tomorrow is never an option. You live in the present, in the now. When have you ever lived in a tomorrow? When you keep putting stuff off for tomorrow, you will never do it. The reason why is because you live in the present, in the now. Do not think other people are going to do everything for you, you will get walked over and passed by your whole life. The only time to do something is now because that is all you live in; tomorrow will never come.

What do I currently expect others to accomplish for me?
What do I keep putting off for tomorrow which I should do now?
What dreams do I want to accomplish but have yet to even start?

Whatever you can do, or dream you can, begin it. Boldness has genius, power and magic in it.
~ Johann Wolfgang von Goethe ~

You will only to be able to finish what you start. Be courageous and begin! Everything in life has to start somewhere; be bold and do it. When you seize the moment, there is a powerful force called genius that is behind it. Commit yourself to what you can do. Hesitating is the root of all failure because you do not even begin. There are all sorts of reasons why someone does not begin something they know they can do or something they dreamed up. It can be anything from fear of ridicule and failure, to making so many excuses as to why they cannot start they end up convincing themselves it was a bad idea before they even begin. If you can dream it, you can do it, all you need to do is begin it!

How has hesitation stopped me from beginning in the past?
What do I dream I can do?
What do I know I can do?

The man who removes a mountain begins by carrying away small stones.
~ Chinese Proverb ~

Some projects are small and some are as big as mountains. You have to start somewhere. Every stone you move takes you one stone closer to removing that mountain. Every task, large or small, has a beginning, middle, and an end. By doing a lot of little tasks, it all adds up to completing one big project. The biggest task you can imagine starts as an idea and then is achieved by hundreds, if not thousands, of small little tasks. These little tasks may appear to be irrelevant, but in the end they add up to something magnificent. It takes a long time to remove a mountain one pebble at time. Likewise, it takes a long time to become established and successful in your field. Do not give up because you have little patience. Cultivate patience. Great things come with time and hard, smart work.

What small task have I done only to create something big?
What was a project I accomplished which I was proud of?
How many little steps did it take to complete it?
State one goal! What small steps do I need to take to accomplish this goal?

Everything you've ever wanted is on the other side of fear.
- George Adair -

Fear is the number one cause that prevents people from reaching their full potential. Seventy-four percent of Americans fear public speaking—more than those who fear death. Most fears come from childhood, adults in our life, and memories of experiences growing up. Fear is a state-of-mind which we chose to cultivate and limits us. Start facing your fears and soon enough, you will no longer fear it. Imagine you just moved into a spacious new home. Think of your comfort zone as a cardboard box you used to move your wardrobe. Within that box is where you reside. Now imagine you're in the box and the box gets placed into storage in your new house—the attic, the basement, or maybe a large closet under the stairs. Because it's comfortable, you stay there. To leave that comfort zone of a box, you will be uncomfortable and have to face numerous fears when you do. But once you do, you will be able to see the magnificent new home you just moved into. You are no longer in storage, you are thriving in the real world.

What is out of my comfort zone?
What have I chosen to be scared to do?
What benefits do I see from facing my fears and going out of my comfort zone?

Life is what happens to you while you're busy making other plans.
- John Lennon -

Do not let life pass you by! Life can go as fast or as slow as you want. When you are sitting at home watching TV, the rest of the world is living life. When you are making plans to live your life, the rest of the world is living life. You can live your life while making plans! Get off the couch and go live your life. If something is holding you back, cut the cord and go live. You have far less than 36,500 days to become the person you want to be if you choose to live to be 100 years young. Don't waste a single day. Stop letting opportunities and experiences pass you by because you are too busy with something else. Get excited that you are alive!!

If I were to die at 100, how many days do I have left?
How many days if I pass away at 80 years young?
How do I see myself living life to the fullest?
(HINT: Use your imagination)
What actions can I realistically do to live life to the fullest?

Either write something worth reading or do something worth writing.
- Benjamin Franklin -

Go out and make something of your life. Do something interesting that someone would want to write about you and what you did so that others would want to read it as well. Go out and do something out of the ordinary. Be and do exceptional things. Live an exciting life. Find your passion, build your desire, and get motivated to go against all odds to create something worth writing about. You can also write a book, write a blog, write an article, something that adds value to others who you are targeting. Anyone can write a book; very few people on the other hand have books written about them. Biographies and autobiographies are about interesting people who lived a life of worth and other people want to dream they can do those things too. Biographies are also a fantastic way to learn from other successful people's mistakes. Live your dreams and create them into reality so others will look at your life with envy as well!

What is something I could write which is worth reading? Be specific!
What have I done already that is worth reading if I or someone else wrote about it?
What can I do in the future that will be worth writing and reading about?

Perfection is not attainable, but if we chase perfection we can catch excellence.
- Vince Lombardi -

Nothing is perfect, especially life. There will always be room for improvement. Since there is always room for improvement, keep striving for perfection. Every day you should be learning not only from your mistakes, but successes as well. Figure out how you can constantly improve in all areas of your life. Never take mediocrity as a way of life. By chasing perfection you are already above everyone else who are content with average or below average. Do your best in everything you do. If you give up or get ticked off because you can not get something perfect, relax, you are approaching, if not have already exceeded, excellence. You can be great, excellent, brilliant, successful, etc. but you can never be perfect. Strive for perfection and obtain excellence. You are your own toughest critic. Take a break from perfection and look at everything you have already done.

What area am I my own worst critic?
What is perfection to me?
Where does excellence come in?
What areas am I excellent in?
(HINT: Ask your friends and family!)

Be miserable. Or motivate yourself. Whatever has to be done, it's always your choice.
- Wayne Dyer -

You are the maker of your own life. Everyday is a choice as to what you will and will not do. Even if the worst of the worst just happened, it is now in the past and you have the choice to be miserable or motivate yourself to turn that negative into a positive. Everyone in the world has more than enough opportunities to be miserable, and yet, only some people motivate themselves to successful actions. Do not be part of the miserable major majority—go make something of yourself. You are the only one with the power to motivate you to become successful. Make the right choice, you know which one that is.

What do I find myself currently choosing?
What or who is enabling me to choose to be miserable?
How can I correct that?
How do I motivate myself?

I have never in my life learned anything from any man who agreed with me.
- Dudley Field Malone -

A person who always agrees or can never say "no" is called a "yes man." When you surround yourself with people who consistently agree with you, you end up learning nothing. When you have people who disagree, it gives you new perspectives. People who agree with you will never question what you say or use their critical thinking skills to come up with different solutions. Surrounding yourself with "yes men" means you have to figure everything out on your own, so there is no use to even have a "yes man" around other than stroking your ego. On the flip side of the coin, it is your responsibility to not be a "yes man" yourself. You need to be able to set boundaries by saying "no." Start asking questions to the authority figures in your life and stand up for your values and principles when the status quo goes against it; the status quo will always be against a free thinker. Always!

How can I surround myself with critical thinkers?
List 5 benefits I get from people who agree with me and 5 from people who disagree with me.
Which column is more appealing and helpful?
Where in my life can I stop agreeing and start questioning?
How can I start saying "no?"

When I was 5 years old, my mother always told me that happiness was the key to life. When I went to school, they asked me what I wanted to be when I grew up. I wrote down 'happy.' They told me I didn't understand the assignment, and I told them they didn't understand life.
- John Lennon -

Some peoples' only dream in life is to be happy. People who are happy have this dream just like people who are miserable have this dream. To become truly happy, you must know what it is that makes you happy. The key to life is happiness. The key to happiness is pursuing what makes you happy, happiness is simply a state-of-mind; it comes from your actions. It is unlikely to live a happy life when you are doing what you hate to do. Even if you love what you do, happiness is not guaranteed. There are numerous areas in your life, when well balanced, you will become happy.

How can I improve my relationships with my friends?
How can I improve my relationships with my family?
How can I improve my financial situation?
How can I improve my physical environment?

How can I improve my career?
How can I improve my social life?
How can I improve my health?
How can I improve my attitude?
How can I improve my personal development?
How can I improve my romance life?
How can I improve my spiritual growth?

What counts is not necessarily the size of the dog in the fight – it's the size of the fight in the dog.
~ Dwight D. Eisenhower ~

The Spartans were only 300 men but they would win battles against thousands. In the battle against Goliath, David won even though he was much smaller than the giant bred for war. In the American Revolution, the colonies had drastically fewer men than the British. The colonists had more to gain and less to lose which gave them more motivation to create a "free country" to live in. You are the same way. It is not your physical size or athleticism that determines what is inside you. Your state of mind can make or break you in any competition in life. Life is a competition no matter how competitive you are. You will win if you believe in yourself and have the strength to persevere through all the battles that life presents to you.

What have I noticed about people who succeed?
When have I beat someone or some team that was "bigger" than me?
What thoughts and skills do I need to build my "fight" inside me?

No masterpiece was ever created by a lazy artist.
~ Anonymous ~

It took Michelangelo four years on his back to paint the Sistine Chapel. Imagine that you spend all day, every day, on your back painting a picture you can not stand back and look at to admire your progress. If he was lazy and cut corners, no one would care about that church. Masterpieces take time and extreme effort. When you think something is good and you are finished, ask yourself if you just created a masterpiece! If you are the average person, the answer will always be no. Put care and effort into everything you do. Do not cut corners and do not accept average when you know you can create greatness. If it takes an extra hour or extra decade, then it takes an extra forty years to create a masterpiece instead of something average which will be forgotten before the end of the day. Masterpieces last forever, they are the closest thing that can reach perfection. Take your time and do not accept average. Strive for excellence!!

What did I create that was not a masterpiece simply because I was lazy?
How do I feel about my finished product after I was lazy about it?
What masterpiece do I want to create?

If you want to achieve greatness, stop asking for permission.
- Anonymous -

This world is crawling with negative, small-minded dream stealers who want nothing more than to stop you from pursuing and reaching your goals. When you ask permission, you will get one of two answers: yes or no. When you do not ask for permission the answer will always be yes. It is better to apologize than it is to ask for permission. It is better to pursue greatness and apologize for taking the initiative than it is to ask for permission and possibly get that no. Once you get a no, that is it. You can still pursue what you wanted but will face more opposition and get in more trouble than if you just do it without asking. When you have small minds around you, never ask for permission, apologize for being great. Apologize for being a free thinker with ambition! Apologize for being awesome!

What did I not pursue because I asked for permission?
What was I able to achieve because I did not ask for permission?
Who do I need to stop asking permission for?
Who do I need to never ask permission from again?

People who succeed have momentum. The more they succeed, the more they want to succeed, and the more they find a way to succeed. Similarly, when someone is failing, the tendency is to get on a downward spiral that can even become a self-fulfilling prophecy.
- Tony Robbins -

Think of rolling a snowball down a hill. It starts out small and slow. As it makes its way down, it gets bigger and goes faster. The bigger it gets, the faster it goes. This goes for both success and failure. You can stop the momentum of both any time with just your thoughts. Expectancy Theory is when you expect something to happen because that is what your past experiences have taught you. Expect to succeed and you will start building the successful momentum needed, and you will find new ways to bring success into your life.

What momentum have I been experiencing?
What new ideas do I have which will bring success?
What thoughts do I need to constantly remind myself of?

You've got to get up every morning with determination if you're going to go to bed with satisfaction.
- George Lorimer -

On average, you have 16 hours each day to do what you need to do to be satisfied with yourself. This is a lot of time, more than enough actually. The night before, before you go to bed, make a list of everything which you need to accomplish the next day. As you accomplish them, cross them off the list. Once a week, pick your day, look at what you accomplished in the previous 7 days and make a list of what you will need to accomplish in the next 7 days. Pick up a Planner Pad Pro and look at it throughout the day, move your schedule around if you need to. Do what you need to do to be overtly satisfied with yourself.

What day of the week will I debrief myself of the previous week and determine what I will need to accomplish in the upcoming week?
What organization system will I implement? (HINT: Do your research!)
What time management system will I implement? (HINT: Do your research!)

**When I let go of what I am,
I become what I might be.**
~ Lao Tzu ~

Who you are right now is a product of your past experiences, the environment you grew up in, the positive or negative people around you, what people told you what you could or could not do, which messages you agree with, and much more. As a baby you knew what you wanted and how to get it. As you grew up, your surroundings shaped you into the person you are now. You would be a different person if you did not listen to your parents or teachers when you were six. That is all in the past now! We all carry negative baggage from the past and it weighs us down and holds us back. Think of your past as an emergency brake in your car. You can still drive with it on, but you will go slower, the drive will be more sluggish, and you'll get burned out. Once you release the emergency brake, let go of your baggage, you allow yourself freedom to move forward and become the person that you want to be, the person you might have been—if not for your baggage. Master Practitioners of Neuro-Linguistic-Programming (NLP), Mental and Emotional Release™ (MER), and/or Time Line Therapy™ specialize in instantly releasing baggage. Look one up!

What baggage am I carrying with me?
What is the number one thing holding me back?
What might I have become if it was not for my past environment?
How can I become that now?

**If you are not willing to risk the usual,
you will have to settle for the ordinary.**
~ Jim Rohn ~

Elon Musk and his partners sold PayPal and netted him $165 million. Elon Musk then risked it all to the point he was borrowing money for rent. When you invest money in the stock market, businesses, real estate, etc., those are all risks. When you ask someone out on a date, you are risking rejection. When you take a test, you risk failure. When you apply for a job, you risk not getting it. If you do not risk anything, you will end up settling for an ordinary life like billions of other people. The wealthy 1% are not ordinary; they are risk takers and deserve every penny while the ordinary people get filled with envy and say they have a right to their successes and bank accounts. The risk Elon Musk took turned multiple businesses into separate multi-billion dollar empires - that's risk. Many successful people risked everything, lost it and risked it all again after working hard to get it back. They are not ordinary because they not only risked everything, they continuously take enormous risks. Being ordinary is safe, boring, and dull. You will never be successful being ordinary, safe, boring, and dull. Take calculated risks!

Last time I took a risk, what good came from it?
What is ordinary in my life?
How can I change that?
What can I risk to become great?

All our dreams can come true if we have the courage to pursue them.
- Walt Disney -
Anything is possible. Everything started as a dream, an idea. We have what we have because someone with a "stupid" idea pursued their vision. They had the courage to stand up against negative people who told them their idea was dumb, impossible, impractical, useless, etc. To become great, you must rise above small-minded, useless dream stealers who gave up on their life and go out and pursue what you were born for. Almost all of the ideas that you have for inventions to change the world or to change your community are great ideas, you just told the wrong people who took away your courage. Every great success story is full of failures and negative small-minded dream stealers who attempt to hold others back. Develop the confidence needed to have the courage to pursue your dreams.

What is my biggest dream for my life or the world?
When have I experienced courage to overcome the dream stealers?
What did I experience when I pursued my dreams?

To be successful, you must accept all challenges that come your way. You can't just accept the ones you like.
- Mike Gafka -
If you keep passing up challenges that scare you or you think are a waste of time, it will take you a lot longer to become successful, if ever. Challenges are opportunities. Life seems unfair in the short-term, but in the long-term it is more than fair, you get what you deserve. Determining the difference between fair and unfair is a biased differentiation between everyone. One thing is certain: it is unwise for you to be picky and only accept the challenges you want. Good and bad things in life will happen. The bad comes to us for a reason and it is unfair to brush it aside. Be fair and wise, and face challenges head on to learn and grow as an individual. Earn the life you are destined for.

What have I passed up because I was too picky?
What is the difference between fair and unfair in terms of my life challenges?
How can I make the unfair, fair?

Our greatest fear should not be of failure, but of succeeding at things in life that don't really matter.
- Francis Chan -
There are a lot of things in life that, in the end, do not matter. You successfully completed watching an entire season of your favorite television show or completed the last level in a video game! Big deal, what do you have to show for it? Nothing

worthwhile. When you try and fail, at least you tried to make something of yourself. When you succeed at tasks without ever failing, then you did not set the bar high enough and it really did not matter. What matters is that you grow as an individual; failure is essential to growth. Success is achieved through continuous failure and perseverance because you are doing something that really matters to real world applications.

What did I succeed at in the past that no longer matters?
What am I currently working on that does not matter in the long run?
What accomplishments do I need to complete so they matter?

You can never cross the ocean until you have the courage to lose sight of the shore.
~ Christopher Columbus ~
You will not experience any accomplishments or make any major breakthroughs unless you are prepared to go out of your comfort zone. Get away from what is familiar and experience new situations to grow as an individual. To move forward in life, you cannot look back and dwell; let the past go and keep your eyes on your "new world." The only thing holding you back is you. The reason why you are holding yourself back is because of what you learned in the past; all those false, negative, limiting beliefs projected upon you by your teachers, parents, friends, coaches, neighbors, family, etc. Let it go and allow yourself to move forward.

What is holding me back from "losing sight of the shore?"
What is waiting for me on the other side of the "ocean?"
What can I do to step out of my comfort zone every day?

The distance between insanity and genius is measured only by success.
~ Bruce Feirstein ~
Recall a time when you were watching someone and thought they were stupid or crazy for trying something, and then when they succeeded, you thought they were genius! This happens frequently to people with limiting beliefs about what is possible. The Wright Brothers were considered insane even after their first flight. What seems insane and pointless to one is a global revolutionary change to another. True genius is not acknowledging that there is a box to think outside of and having the courage to go out and do what no one else will. People who think something is insane do not even try; a genius will try until they succeed. Along the path of failure, the genius will always be termed insane by the same group of people. When someone says you are doing something insane which you believe is a great idea, thank them and pat yourself on the back; you are on the right track.

What idea do I have that is crazy enough to be genius?
What insane idea did I stop pursuing but know it is a genius idea?
What insane thing did I accomplish to be considered a genius?

What's the point of being alive if you don't at least try to do something remarkable?
- Anonymous -

You were given this wonderful life where you choose to do and be anything you want. Yet, the majority of people spend 37 hours a week on average watching television. This is equivalent to a full-time job that's not only wasting your life away, it fills your head with some of the worst garbage you can consume, especially if you're American. Reality television is the most destructive. Have some respect for yourself, turn off the TV and read a book. Successful people watch less than 7 hours of TV a week, do not watch reality shows, and read for one hour a day. The average person puts on commercial radio; successful people listen to self-improvement audio books. We are all destined for greatness, but it is your choice to waste your life in front of a TV or to do something remarkable with your time. Trying and failing is way better than not trying at all. Most people will never try. Be remarkable and have the courage to try everything you can dream of.

What TV shows am I willing to give up for greatness?
For how many hours per week?
What is something remarkable I have not tried yet?
What are my replacement activities for TV, video games, movies, social media, fiction books and alcohol/drugs?

You can't fall if you don't climb. But there's no joy in living your whole life on the ground.
- Anonymous -

We can all agree on the first statement that if you do not climb, there is no chance for you to fall. Imagine going rock climbing with friends, but you do not climb. You watch them climb higher and higher, take risks, and laugh. After some time they make it to the top of the cliff and disappear over the edge. They made it to the top—and you are still on the ground with the rest of the average world. You can transfer this metaphor to every area of life. If you do not climb out of your comfort zone, face your fears, and take risks, you will always be on the ground watching everyone else rise to success. You, and only you, can make the choice to start climbing and get off the ground. Life on the ground is boring and full of complainers who gave up. You're better than that and you know it!

What "cliff" do I want to "climb?"
How have I been living my life on the ground?
What was my greatest success?
What risks did I take?

Twenty years from now you will be more disappointed by the things that you didn't do than by the ones you did do. So throw off the bowlines. Sail away from the safe harbor. Catch the trade winds in your sails. Explore! Dream! Discover!

- Mark Twain -

Think about what you wanted to do years ago which you never attempted to even try. You could be living the benefits of that by now. Most regrets come from not doing something rather than doing something and making a huge mistake. When you "throw off the bowlines" you untie your emotional baggage from the past, allowing you to fearlessly explore avenues you never would have before. After you "sail away from the safe harbor" you put yourself in situations which are uncomfortable and scare you. When something scares you, that is the perfect chance for you to face your fears. By facing your fears, you will grow and become a stronger person, ready for pure greatness!

What did I quit that I wish I had seen through to the end?
What is stopping me from trying it today?
How can I get past those obstacle(s)?
What area(s) of life have I always wanted to explore?
What are three dreams I want to make reality in my life?

Be who you are and say what you feel, because those who mind don't matter and those who matter don't mind.

- Dr. Seuss -

There has never been, nor will ever be, someone like you. You are you! Be proud of that. When you speak your mind, you will naturally have people who agree with you and people who disagree with you. Those who choose to be offended are irrelevant to your life; they chose to put themselves in the category of those who do not matter. The people who disagree with you but respect your opinion are the ones who truly matter. They accept you for you! When you speak openly about how you feel and people "mind," they will try to push their flawed agendas on you, believing you are wrong; these people do not matter. The people who matter do not have to agree with you, but they will respect you and your feelings. Be the person you were meant to be.

How did I handle myself last time someone disagreed with my feelings?
How do those that matter versus those that do not matter make me feel?
What is keeping those that do not matter in my life?
How can I correct this situation?

The first step toward success is taken when you refuse to be a captive of the environment in which you first find yourself.

- Mark Caine -

Settling for what you get is not the action of successful people. Mediocrity is not an option. If you find yourself in the lower class, middle class, or even the lower/

middle part of the upper class, do not feel like that is where you belong. Do not be held prisoner of your current social or financial status. If you are unsatisfied with the environment in which you grew up or find yourself now, do not accept it and be a prisoner of mediocrity. You are the only one in the world who can change your environment into what you want it to be. Refuse to be average, refuse the typical mindset of popular belief that being regular is a good thing. Being regular is not a good thing! Be uncommon, unusual, extreme, strange, rare, unique and special. Be an individual! Be the best version of YOU that YOU can be!

> What environment have I found myself captive in?
> What environment would I like to see myself in?
> What are the first couple steps I need to take?

You must be the change you want to see in the world.
- Mohandas Gandhi -

Talk is cheap. Stop being a hypocrite! Confront your Jungian Shadow (you'll learn more if you look this up yourself)! It is easy to tell people how to act but the most powerful way to get people to act the way you want them to is by acting that way yourself. People have scientifically proven to follow the method of "monkey see, monkey do" unless their values and willpower supersede their surroundings. When we see someone do something, it is more likely that we will do it, even if it is wrong. The greatest leaders in the world lead by example because they know the power that comes with it. We learn by osmosis! Mother Theresa and the Dalai Lama brought peace to millions through leading by example; not just talking.

> How do the leaders in my life act?
> Do they lead by example or are they hypocrites?
> What actions can I take today to be that change I want to see?
> How will my actions look from a third person perspective?
> What will they think, see, hear, feel?

Keep on going and the chances are you will stumble on something, perhaps when you are least expecting it. I have never heard of anyone stumbling on something sitting down.
- Charles F. Kettering -

When you keep trying and keep moving forward, you will eventually succeed, even in ways you did not plan. Continually trying opens up new opportunities. When you do not do anything, you will always get nothing. How can you get a job that you do not apply for? You have to apply and interview. If you really want the job you have to make follow-up phone calls and send thank you letters. By not doing anything you will produce and receive nothing. Always keep trying and good things will happen; sometimes faster than expected and sometimes years longer than you had hoped for. As long as you keep going and never quit, you will accomplish all your goals that you set out for yourself; some way, some how!

What have I stumbled upon after endless tries to succeed?
What have I accomplished from not doing anything?
What have I received when I least expected it after endless attempts?

I find that the harder I work, the more luck I seem to have.
- Thomas Jefferson -

There is no such thing as luck. The luckiest people in the world work extremely hard to create their luck. You can think of luck as opportunities which present themselves. The only way you will get opportunities is by working for them. The trickiest part is when an opportunity presents itself, you have to take advantage of it every time. That is not luck whatsoever. Create your own luck by working hard everyday and be ready to take advantage of them every time. The more opportunities you see and act on, the luckier you will be. Success is like a snowball, it starts out small and slow but as it rolls down the hill it will get bigger and go faster. Work smart and hard for "luck" will follow.

What luck did I receive from hard, smart work?
What luck do I want to have happen to me?
What do I need to do to make that luck happen?
What beliefs do I need to correct to live a luckier life?

Eighty percent of success is showing up.
- Woody Allen -

Too many times people do not show up somewhere because it is: raining, snowing, too cold, too hot, too tired, too busy, too hungry, it's the holiday, it's the weekend, or too full, to show up. Of course there are many more excuses which people have used. But don't make excuses! Excuses come from the tongues of losers, not winners. The simple act of just showing up is 80% of success because that is the starting point. When you show up, you are there to receive opportunities. When you show up, you give yourself the opportunity to progress in life. Decide what is important to you and show up at everything which will benefit what is important to you. Look at your choices as an investment of your time, what will progress your life forward most? You will be glad you did. If you are not impressed by your first or hundredth time of showing up, try something different. Keep showing up!

What great experience came from showing up?
What great experience came from showing up after not wanting to go?
What do I not want to show up to anymore? Why?
What activity will I replace it with?

Motivation is what gets you started. Habit is what keeps you going.
- Jim Ryun -

Create the habit of being constantly motivated. Make it your usual, routine, habitual behavior to be eager to keep giving yourself reasons to act or work in a productive way. When you have good work habits, there is no stopping you once you get started. Success is inevitable.

What am I motivated to start?
What good habits will keep me going?
What bad habits do I need to correct?

People often say that motivation doesn't last. Well, neither does bathing – that's why we recommend it daily.
- Zig Ziglar -

Intrinsic motivation comes from within you, from being inspired. Extrinsic motivation comes from outside factors and elements. Then there is motivation towards which means you get motivated to receive something. Motivation away is when you get motivation to keep a specific outcome from forming. Everyday you get the motivation to do something, anything. To keep doing that action, you have to keep getting motivated. Motivation is temporary, that is why you have to get motivated everyday. Inspiration, on the other hand, is what lasts. When you are inspired to do something, possess the Intrinsic Motivation Towards, your motivation will be greater than you can imagine. Nothing will ever stop you!

List everything I have intrinsic motivation towards to do!
List everything I have external motivation away?
How can I turn my extrinsic motivation away into intrinsic motivation towards?

You may have to fight a battle more than once to win it.
- Margaret Thatcher -

Do not expect to succeed the first time you try something. Expect to learn from everything you do on how to do it better the next time around. Life is not a one-chance-and-done type deal. Even with working for a strict boss, you will get a second chance at least one time during your employment, hopefully. Never give up. Always learn from your mistakes. Your life is like a war, you can fight all the battles you want as many times as you want to win the war. Succeed at life through constant repetition until you succeed.

What "battle" did I give up on after losing the first time around?
What "battle" have I won after trying a second or hundredth time?
How can I prepare myself to win "the war"?

BOOK THREE

If the facts don't fit the theory, change the facts.
- Albert Einstein -

This goes hand in hand with "perception is interpretation." Whatever you believe to be true, you will find the evidence to support. No matter what you believe, you will look at something as factual to back up that belief. When you start looking at the facts differently, you will see more opportunity in your life. You can change the evidence the world gives you by looking at it differently, thus changing the facts.

What facts did I receive which do not support my theory of success?
How can I look at the above "facts" differently to turn them into opportunity?
What can I learn from my stated facts?

Stop trying to leave, and you will arrive. Stop seeking, and you will see. Stop running away, and you will be found.
- Lao Tzu -

There is no better place for you to be than where you are right now, every time. A great deal of people end up leaving before they even arrive, right before the moment of accomplishment. You may have experienced being on an endless search for answers outside of yourself only to realize the answers you were searching for were within you the entire time. Or you may have tried to avoid a situation by running away, whether it was your job, relationships, finances, health, etc. You are your own worst enemy, as well as, your own greatest asset. Take the advice from Lao Tzu and get out of your own way to find what your are looking for in life.

How do I sabotage myself?
What can I do differently?
What makes me my greatest asset?
What am I currently looking for?
How will I arrive?

If you're not stubborn, you'll give up on experiments too soon. And if you're not flexible, you'll pound your head against the wall and you won't see a different solution to a problem you're trying to solve.
- Jeff Bezos -

Stick with your initial vision of why you started and be flexible on how you manifest that vision. Jeff Bezos, the founder of Amazon.com, says, "The thing about inventing is you have to be both stubborn and flexible, more or less simultaneously. The hard part is figuring out when to be which!" Whether or not you are an inventor, entrepreneur, student, or employee, it is ideal to be stubborn and flexible when necessary. Be open to suggestions from others when needed to get past the roadblocks which your stubbornness can't troubleshoot.

What happened when I was stubborn for too long?
What happened when I was flexible?
How can I be more stubborn and flexible next time?

If you do what you always did, you will get what you always got.
~ Albert Einstein ~

Albert Einstein defined insanity as doing the same thing and expecting different results. When you keep doing the same things, you will always get the same results. To produce different results you need to do something different. When something does not work out, you receive feedback throughout the process and at the end of it. You are insane to think that if you do it again the same way you will produce different results. There are a lot of insane people out there, stop being one of them. If you keep getting into bad relationships, chances are you are doing the same thing when you start those relationships. If you are tired of living paycheck to paycheck, try saving, investing, cutting your expenses, and getting another source of income. This concept fits all areas of life.

What were my actions that produced the results with which I am living today?
What undesired results do I keep producing?
How can I change them?
What feedback have I received so I can change my actions next time?

Enjoy the little things, for one day you may look back and realize they were the big things.
~ Robert Breault ~

When you go through life, you may not even know when something big happens; in the cases you do, you probably will remember them forever. On the other hand, its natural to rarely notice all the little things that life has to offer. Our minds think in pictures and feelings. As you grow older, you will remember that some of the best feeling memories are pictures of the little things that did not seem to matter at the time. Just like action steps, the little things add up into big things. Gain appreciation for everything that happens to you in life. Little things do matter, they are what add up to big things. Slow life down and appreciate everything from the sky on down to a bug; from your parents to a stranger you bumped into on the street. Life goes as fast as you let it. Slow down and take it all in.

What little things in my past do I appreciate now that I did not before?
What little things can I put more appreciation towards now?
What state of mind do I need to start appreciating everything?
(Even the negatives!)

Everything has beauty, but not everyone can see.
~ Confucius ~

We are programmed in today's society to judge everything by its looks. When you go into a job interview, you want to look your best. When you buy flowers, you want to buy the best-looking ones. When people buy jewelry it is because of the physical beauty. Beauty is deeper than that. Everything is beautiful because of what they stand for and what they do. Every person is beautiful because of what is inside them, it is who they are. Stop looking at the bad and all the flaws in others and in life. If you look for them, you will see them. Start looking beneath the surface at what is good. Life is full of beauty!

How do I feel when I am judged for my outer appearance?
What first impression did I get from something because of the outer appearance which turned out to be false?
Think of something I hate. What beauty lies within it?

Happiness is a butterfly, which when pursued, is always beyond your grasp, but which, if you will sit down quietly, may alight upon you.
~ Nathaniel Hawthorne ~

Happiness is not a destination to strive for. It is a state of mind, a way of life. You live and experience happiness. Do not strive for and pursue happiness, it will always be just beyond your grasp. One way to be happy is to slow life down, relax, get to know who you are and what you want and you may become happy just doing that. Happiness is a state of mind and you can choose to be happy, angry, or sad. That simple! Research happiness and how you can reach that state of mind faster than you can from the results of your dieting, workout routine, and investments. Stop pursuing happiness and simply be happy. Your thoughts control your emotions; have happy thoughts and you will be happy. Make the choice to be happy and simply, be happy!

What makes me happy when I think about it?
What activities make me happy?
What accomplishments will make me happy?

Every truth passes through three stages before it is recognized. In the first, it is ridiculed. In the second, it is opposed. In the third, it is regarded as self evident.
~ Arthur Schopenhauer ~

Before any new idea of truth takes critical mass, it goes through these three stages. It is ridiculed because it is against the norm. It is hard for people to comprehend that there is a new and better way to do things other than what they have been doing their whole life. When opposition sets in, everyone around does not want to accept it as the new norm. Last, critical mass takes hold. This is the goal with almost every new idea or concept presented. The Wright Brothers with the airplane, Henry Ford with the V-8 engine, Thomas Edison with the light bulb, Bill Gates with the PC, Steve Jobs with the smart-phone, Galileo's astronomical observations, and the list goes on. All greatness surpasses these three necessary stages.

What truth have I ridiculed before I knew the whole story?

What truth did I oppose, or still oppose? For what reason?
How did I get past the ridicule and opposition?

The only thing worse than a man you can't control is a man you can.
- Margo Kaufman -

When you can be controlled it means you are weak, you have no confidence or self-esteem. Your self worth depends on what others make you do. When it comes to dating and the opposite sex, it is highly unattractive to be controllable except for those who look for that in a significant other. It may be fun for someone to control you and they will keep you around for that reason only; their level of respect for you will not be that of something of worth. Puppets bring no challenges, fun, excitement, new experiences, passion, etc. If you are the puppet, get a clue and end that part of your life with tact and grace. If you are the puppet master, have some decency and stop being wickedly manipulative.

What areas am I the puppet and the puppet master?
What situation have I experienced when I was more attracted to someone who did not obey my every command? Why?
What situation have I experienced when I was more attracted to someone who I could control every step of the way? Why?

You must be willing to go inside yourself, to learn to maximize the mind, go where you have never been before.
- Jim Lutes -

Notice all the opportunities life has to offer. Your thoughts and actions bring these opportunities to you, so why not take advantage of them? Deep down, your subconscious knows exactly what you need to do to become what you want. To access it, go where you may have never been before, inside yourself for an honest "heart-to-heart" to find what you're searching for. Decide to create situations to help you "wake up" and begin taking advantage of what you learn about yourself. Start noticing everything around you and how you are affected by it. Realize you have a lot more potential than you are giving yourself credit for. Awaken your awareness by learning how to maximize the mind, a great starting point is NLP. In order to get to places you have never been before, you first have to go places you have never been before, inside yourself. To achieve anything, it all starts in the mind.

What gives me motivation?
What opportunities do I see now that I passed up before?
What opportunities do I presently see in my life?
How can I take advantage of them?

Some men see things as they are and say why – I dream things that never were and say why not.
- George Bernard Shaw -

Our attitudes can either help us or hinder us in creating the life of our dreams. It is far more empowering and creative to go through life being open to possibilities, than to adopt a cynical attitude, criticizing and being negative. Those who choose to look upon the world with wonder and say "why not?" embrace hope and faith, allow for new possibilities, and enable dreams to become reality. Cynics and small-minded people who doubt and denigrate cannot see possibilities and close off the ability to grow and improve themselves and the world. Whenever you find yourself being fearful, critical, or doubting, try adopting the opposite attitude and ask yourself "why not?" Listen and watch the answers unfold.

> What situations have I been the small thinker by asking "why"?
> What dreams do I have that I should ask "why not"?
> What dreams have I had which never were?
> "Why not" make it a reality?

Every thought we think is creating our future.
~ Louise L. Hay ~

Our thoughts, our imagination, is incredibly powerful. Neuroscience proves that when you imagine doing a specific task, the same neurons in your brain "light up" as if you were physically doing it. Imagining yourself doing a project for one hour is equivalent to eight hours of physical labor. Dr. Biasiotto at the University of Chicago studied this principle with basketball players. Players who physically practiced their basketball free throws for 30 days increased their success rate by 24%. Yet players who only visualized making their shots, without actually physically practicing, increased their success rate by 23%. Double your success rate by using the power of your thoughts with action! Use your imagination to see in your mind what you desire to see, hear what you want to hear, and feel what want to feel! By consistently thinking positively, our actions will begin to naturally follow suit. Thinking about thinking is what separates the one percenters from everyone else, that is what *The Secret* is!

> What do I want to become real in my life?
> What will I see, hear, and feel?
> What is the ideal time of day for me to visualize?
> For how long? (Realistically)

I think and think for months and years. Ninety-nine times, the conclusion is false. The hundredth time I am right.
~ Albert Einstein ~

Like machines running 24/7 our thoughts, mind, and subconscious are extremely powerful. Albert Einstein, math and physics genius, understood that our initial thoughts are often wrong. Experiment with everything and test different theories while never giving up. The longer you concentrate on solving a problem, the more likely it is that you will come up with the correct answer. To come up with the answer you are searching for, continue forward, keep trying and calibrate your thoughts based on feedback you get. Remember that you may be wrong 99 times before you are right. Just don't give up!

How quickly do I give up?
How long do I think about something before doing it?
How long should I contemplate?
What do I need to keep experimenting on until I obtain the outcome I desire?

Logic will get you from A to B. Imagination will take you everywhere.
- Albert Einstein -

Anyone can find where to go by following a step-by-step blueprint. It takes real creativity and imagination to figure out a different path to overcome obstacles that arise. When you can come up with new ways to do something, you will bypass "B" and go straight to the top. Most of the world has a set way of doing something and do not falter from it, even when there is a better way. Find that better way and rise above everyone else in life.

What am I doing to entertain my creative imagination?
How often do I meditate?
What benefits will meditation bring in my life? (HINT: Research)
What can I do to break free from the conformed societal thinking?

Positive anything is better than negative thinking.
- Elbert Hubbard -

Negative thinking will never bring you positive anything. There is a mind-body connection and your thoughts directly affect your whole body. When you consistently have negative thoughts, especially about other people, your subconscious perceives it to be true about you. The saying "I am rubber you are glue, what you say bounces off me and sticks to you" is more true than you realize. What you think and say about people comes right back to you and your subconscious believes it to be true only about you. All your positive and negative thinking directly affects your life. Negative thoughts have great potential to wear the body down. Stress is all in the mind but the body responds by restricting blood vessels, aches and pains, losing hair, becoming nauseated, feeling restless, breaking bones, etc. Your thoughts have a direct correlation to how your body reacts and feels.

List at least 20 positive things in my life!
What happened to me after just one hour of positive thinking? How did I feel?
How is positive anything better than negative thinking? (Don't rewrite what is above)

Thinking should become your capital asset, no matter whatever ups and downs you come across in your life.
- Dr. Avul Kalam -

If you are lacking in one of any of the departments in life, your thoughts will help you acquire whatever it is you need. When you hit rock bottom, it is your thoughts that will help you climb out and rise to the top. Throughout life, there will be highs and lows. At times you will be successful and win, and other times you will fail and hit rock bottom. Thoughts are things. Thinking how you can be more successful or how you can get yourself out of a jam is the only thing you have. Thinking about thinking is your best asset.

When have my thoughts proved to be an asset?
What thoughts do I need to acquire to deem them as assets?
Whether I am up or down, what thoughts do I need to thrive?

The only limits in our life are those we impose on ourselves.
~ Bob Proctor ~
Nothing in life is perfect. There are faults and limitations everywhere which you will see only if you are looking for them. When people shop for a car, they look for faults instead of seeing a vehicle that will get you from point A to point B. When shopping for a home, people hire inspectors who are trained in finding every fault they can. If they did not hire an inspector they would never know there were faults until they moved in (hire an inspector before closing to save tens of thousands of dollars in repairs). People who complain, blame others and make excuses for themselves are professional fault finders, nothing is up to standard and they will let the world know it. Drastically improve your life by eliminating the false limitations which we have come to believe as true.

What is one "Limit" I can think of in my life?
How can I view it as a positive?
What past experience makes me see faults rather than the positive?
In what ways will my life improve when I stop looking for my "Limit"?

You are today where your thoughts have brought you; you will be tomorrow where your thoughts take you.
~ James Allen ~
It is nobody's fault but your own pertaining to where you are in life right now. You can blame other people, make all the excuses you can think of, and complain about everything that has happened, but the reality is that your life is what it is because of the thoughts you had. Thoughts are things! The only thing that is guaranteed in life besides the law of physics is that you control your thoughts and your thoughts determine your actions. Your actions, added up, created the life that you are living in right now. The thoughts you have today, right now, will determine what your actions will be once you finish reading this page. Those actions you take, or do not take, will determine who and where you will be tomorrow. Take 100% responsibility for your life starting with your thoughts.

What thoughts did I have which brought me to where I am today?

What thoughts do I need to take me to where I want to be tomorrow?
How can I start taking more responsibility for my life?

Hold a thought for just 17 seconds and the Law of Attraction kicks in. Hold a thought for 68 seconds and things move; manifestation has begun.
- Abraham Hicks -

When you hold a thought in your mind for 17 seconds, positive or negative, you start attracting similar energy into your life whether you want it or not. By concentrating on that one thought for 68 seconds, thats when the Universe starts to move and make things happen for you. This is pure metaphysics which predates Aristotle. If this information is still being suggested by the world's top experts after thousands of years, there should be no doubt in anyone's mind that this is the number one success tool there is! Break free from the conformed Western mindset and start building success skills which have been written about for thousands of years.

What have I manifested from the Law of Attraction?
What can I concentrate on for 68 seconds?
What does my desired result look, feel, and sound like?

It's time to stop tiptoeing around the pool and jump into the deep end, head first. It's time to think big, want more, and achieve it all!
- Mark Victor Hansen -

When you are about to do something worth your time and energy, would it be better to make it amazing or to make it something that people won't even notice? Look in the history books, everyone worth mentioning did something big, not small or average. Have you ever heard the phrase, "go big or go home?" Apply it to everything you do. Dive in head first! No matter what you think, time will pass by, the sun will rise tomorrow, new billionaires will continuously be made, and you will still have thoughts running through your mind. What you think you become, so why not think the best of the best and expect to achieve it all? Do not choose to have the small negative thoughts dominate your mind so you're constantly tiptoeing around the pool. Choose to have big empowering positive thoughts control your mind and take over the deep end of that pool called life.

What big thoughts do I have?
What small thoughts have stopped me in the past?
How can I become an even bigger thinker?

Instead of thinking outside the box, get rid of the box.
- Deepak Chopra -

The statement "thinking outside the box" is a metaphor for thinking differently. Growing up, we are expected to live inside the box of society which is tightly wrapped with the red tape of rules, laws, and regulations. To become more creative, find your voice, live your passions, and fulfill your purpose, it will be easier for you if you do not even acknowledge the existence of "the box." After you unwrap all the red tape and other limitations, you look into this overcrowded box to see everyone acting and thinking the same way. No one is an individual even though they all say they are. Those who do not even know what "the box" looks like are the ones who are living their dreams. They are the ones who employ the "in the box" population. Become your own free thinking person and develop your own beliefs, not the dictated beliefs of the status quo.

What are my creative ideas?
How can I cut the red tape and get out of the box?
How has my life improved by going against the status quo?

We can easily forgive a child who is afraid of the dark; the real tragedy of life is when men are afraid of the light.
- Plato -

A child being afraid of the dark is typical and expected. Parents buy a nightlight or leave the door open with the hallway light on before the child can "safely" go to sleep. On the other hand, it is typical for an adult to be afraid to come out and show the world what they are made of. As an adult, "staying in the dark" is safe because you don't have to face your fears and step into the light. To most people, it is better to hide in the safe dark place than it is to face their fears, step into the light, and risk embarrassment. If being embarrassed is your biggest fear, dedicate one day to doing anything you might see as embarrassing. Go to another city or town to lower the risk if it makes you feel a little better. Develop the strength and courage to face your fears and step into the light, the world needs you to do this, you need you to do this.

How am I avoiding "the light"?
What am I doing to step into "the light"?
What fears do I need to overcome?
How can I do that?

Our lives begin to end the day we become silent about things that matter.
- Martin Luther King Jr. -

Start fighting for the things you believe in. The day we silence our voice on things that truly matter to us is the day our lives no longer have any meaning. Use your voice to speak out against the world and all the wrongs that are happening which you are passionate about changing. Stop talking amongst your friends and use your voice to speak to the world. The term "voice" comes from Dr. Stephen Covey in his book *The 8 Habit*. When you are silent and do not use your voice, you become other people's puppet. Do not let the things that matter to you pass you by because you allowed some "puppet master" to pull your strings. Speak out for or against them. That could mean your boss, family, friends, teacher, neighborhood, community, city, nation...the world! Speak out and be heard instead of talking sheepishly behind their backs!

What are the things that matter to me?
What wrongs do I see within the scope of what matters to me?
How can I use my voice to change the wrongs?

The quickest way to acquire self-confidence is to do exactly what you are afraid to do.
- Anon -

The two most common fears are public speaking and spiders. If you are afraid of public speaking, join a local Toastmasters club and take on leadership roles in your life where you will have to speak. If you are afraid of spiders, start catching them and let them crawl on you, they already take that liberty when you are asleep. For every fear that you have, there are millions of people out there who absolutely love it. For everything you absolutely love to do, there are millions of people out there who are debilitatingly petrified by it. Fear is a state-of-mind just like confidence and happiness. To gain confidence, do what you are afraid to do. Within time, it will no longer be a fear, it may even turn into something you look forward to doing. All achievement will always lie outside your comfort zone and deep within your fears.

What am I afraid to do?
How will I conquer that fear?
What are all the possibilities my life will have after I conquer that fear?

Courage is resistance to fear, mastery of fear - not absence of fear.
- Mark Twain -

The difference between a hero and everyone else is that when faced with fear, they remain calm and do what is right no matter how petrified they are. Fear is there in all of us, the courageous heroes are masters of it. The best way to overcome fear is to face your fears. Seek out activities which elicit fear inside you. When you get use to building up your courage and facing your fears, you will see that you will eventually be doing that in all areas of life. Having courage does not mean to be fearless, it means that you remain calm when you have the fear and do what needs to be done. Master your fear by conquering everything you are afraid of. Develop resistance to it!

How did I face my fears in the past? What did I do?
What fears have I mastered?
What fears will I face in the future with courage?

When I dare to be powerful - to use my strength in the service of my vision, then it becomes less and less important whether I am afraid.
- Audre Lorde -

When soldiers go to war and enter battle, they are afraid. They keep moving forward and seeking the enemy because of their vision for peace. They face their fears to protect their country and the people living in them. In the grand scheme of things, what a soldier fears is not important at all compared to the purpose and future they are fighting for. War is a hellish event which no one should endure, but sadly enough, it is necessary to bring peace. Begin to visualize the life you want to live, the life that you deserve to live. Through visualization, you will build the strength to overcome your fears, because in the end, your fears do not matter compared to the success that is yet to come.

What is my vision?
What am I afraid of to make my vision a reality?
What is the difference between my fears and my vision?

The battles that count aren't the ones for gold medals. The struggles within yourself–the invisible battles inside all of us–that's where it's at.
- Jesse Owens -
As you practice something, whether it is a sport or a speech, the struggles within yourself is what truly matters in the end. As Dr. Stephen Covey puts it, it is the private victory. You have battles you must conquer within yourself to grow. You may win the gold medal but still have not won the invisible battle that is going on inside your head. Conquer your fears and do what is right. Be moral and ethical and you will start winning your inside battles. Face your fears and overcome them to win even more internal battles which no one will ever see. We do not have glass heads, we do not know what is going on inside the minds of other people just like they cannot see the battles inside you. Overcome the struggles within yourself to win at life.

What battles am I facing within myself?
What internal struggles do I need to conquer?
What internal private victories am I proud of?

Life shrinks or expands in proportion to one's courage.
- Anais Nin -
Watch children and notice how they are naturally courageous. They have the courage to do anything they want without fear because "they do not know better." As they grow up, parents, teachers, and friends will shrink that courage by telling them what is and is not safe to do according to their flawed opinion. Once a child is told not to do something, their courage for doing it is taken away. As you experience things on your own, you begin to realize things that never crossed your mind before and that knowledge will either shrink or expand your courage. You may have the courage to skydive for the first time and on the landing you end up breaking your nose or ankle which shrinks your courage to do it again. On the other hand, that same instance could expand your courage because you want to be able to make a perfect landing exactly where the target is.

What experience shrunk my courage?
What experience expanded my courage?
What would I like to have courage to do?

That which doesn't kill us makes us stronger.
- Friedrich Nietzsche -

You may have heard this countless times. It is more true than you can imagine. Every time you survive something, as long as you learn from it, it makes you stronger. Think of your immune system—every time you beat the cold or flu, your immune system is stronger than before and you will not get sick by that same strain of virus. Life is the same way. When you learn something new from experience, you become a stronger individual. You can build confidence, self-esteem, awareness, skills, lessons, etc. Use what life hands you as a way to build yourself up stronger for the next exciting venture life will hand you.

What experience made me a stronger individual?
How did that experience make me stronger? List 5 reasons why!
What have I done after becoming stronger which I never would have done before that incident?

Do one thing every day that scares you.
- Mary Schmich -

Take this to heart. Live it like it is an immutable law of nature. When something scares you, do it. You know it is the right thing to do but something deep down is holding you back because you are scared; this is when you must do it. Facing your fears head on builds confidence, skills, experiences, opportunities and it is a good habit to be in. It is scary to jump off a diving board for the first time. When you do make that jump you realize it was not so bad. You get out of the pool and do it again. The more you do it, the more fun you have. You may even start doing flips and different dives to make it more fun. Everything is scary the first time you do it. Through constant repetition you can overcome any fear.

What fears have I overcame?
What fears will I start facing?
What is the best thing that can happen from facing my fears?

Successful people are always looking for opportunities to help others. Unsuccessful people are always asking, what's in it for me?
- Brain Tracy -

It is human nature to want to help people. In this world, it is easy to become enamored by self-interest, glory, fame, wealth, and power. We may start out being motivated by our nature to help others, but we need to stay self-aware and keep our focus on others as a priority, and not worry about what's in it for ourselves. When we stay focused on others, lasting rewards come to us naturally. History is full of people who lost their focus on caring for others first. Even criminals like Adolf Hitler, Al Capone, and Bernie Madoff all started out being motivated by doing something to help others. But they made the mistake of allowing their own self-interest to take over. They made choices out of integrity with what was right, and became criminals who ultimately paid for their mistakes. Without integrity, success is short lived.

What opportunities do I have to help others?
What results did I receive from the "what's in it for me" mentality?
How have successful people helped me?
How can I find a successful person to help me?

We do not want to gain at someone else's loss; we want to gain while helping the other person to also gain.
~ Jose Silva ~

Purposefully gaining from someone else's loss is the opposite of integrity. It would be nice if it was common for people to help those gain back what they lost rather than profit from it. Even if there is a point when you consciously gain from someone else's loss, it is your integrity which guides you to helping them gain back what was once lost. When you help other people succeed in their endeavors, you gain in miraculous ways. You will begin experiencing a happier, healthier, and more fulfilled life through helping others the best way you know how. This can be perceived as being selfishly selfless. Be selfish by gaining from doing selfless acts. The most successful people help others gain through books, blogs, audios, videos, programs, workshops, seminars, speaking, mentoring, advising, consulting, coaching, teaching, training, etc. The list goes on with each particular person and how they specifically help people gain using their own knowledge, skills, and expertise.

How have I helped others gain?
What have I gained from helping others?
How can I help someone gain in the near future?

When I stand before God at the end of my life, I would hope that I would not have a single bit of talent left and could say, I used everything you gave me.
~ Erma Bombeck ~

Religious or not, this is a great life quote to live by. Develop the talents that you have and use them to the best of your ability. Leave nothing left when you come to the end of your life. Your life can end before you wake up tomorrow! In the middle of the day and at the end of the day ask yourself what more you can do. What you can do better! You have a lot of talent because you are human. If you do not believe you have a talent then you are not using everything you have. Stop wasting your life and wasting your talents; that is one regret you do not want to have when the time comes. When you think you are done and gave it your all, think again. There is always more to do and always more ways to improve. Make it a daily effort.

What are my talents?
What talents do I use daily?
What talents am I neglecting?

An eye for eye only ends up making the whole world blind.
~ Mohandas Gandhi ~

"An eye for an eye, a tooth for a tooth." Revenge is when someone does something bad to you, so to make yourself feel better you go out and do the same thing right back to them. Vengeance and retaliation doesn't work. When people say, "be the bigger person," that means to rise above vengeance. End it right there and forgive. Forgiving does not mean you have to forget, it simply means to let it go. Forgiveness is for you, not for the person who wronged you. If everyone had an "eye-for-an-eye" mentality there would be never-ending war and violence. While it is extremely common today, and it may seem that this is reality as we know it, the truth is, forgiveness is evident everywhere. Look around and you will see people forgive, and not retaliate. That is the correct way to a better world.

Who do I need to forgive?
What good has retaliation brought into my life?
What areas did I see improvement on after true forgiveness took place?

The only way to have a friend is to be one.
- Ralph Waldo Emerson -

You can not expect people to treat you in a way that you do not treat others. Treat others the way you want to be treated. This is especially hard when you are being treated unfairly and contrary to the way you treat them. Friends may appear to be friends only to use you until you helped them. They may owe you money, steal your significant other, borrow a movie, etc. Stay true to your morals and treat everyone the way you want to be treated. You gain friends by being friendly, by treating them as friends. You will never get a friend after treating someone horribly, like they are less than human. Be a friend to everyone, be empathetic and understanding to their situations and you will win new friends every day.

How did I act when a friend did not treat me like a friend?
How do I want to be treated from a friend?
How should I conduct myself to make that happen?
What situations did I not treat someone like a friend?
How can I make it right?

You make a living by what you earn; you make a life by what you give.
- Winston Churchill -

Earning money is termed "making a living." Yet what matters more than money is what you give on your journey in life. You will be remembered by the legacy you leave behind, what you have given to your children, your community, the world. Giving comes in many forms. It could be by volunteering with a nonprofit which speaks to your heart. What and how you give is of greater worth than the money donated. Thomas Edison and Steve Jobs are not remembered for their bank accounts. They are remembered for their inventions they gave to the world. Yes, they earned livings from them, too. But it was in their giving that the worth, the lasting value, was found. If money was of greater value, if everyone thought only about money and what is best for themselves, there would be no giving of any kind. Focus on what you can give, and the money will come as a byproduct.

What have I given so far to help the greater community?
What can I give to help the greater community?
What do I want to be remembered for when I am gone?
How can I do that?

A verbal attack on you has absolutely nothing to do with you, it belongs to your attacker.
~ Jim Britt ~

If everyone likes you, you are doing something really wrong. The great thing about life is that we are all different and have all sorts of perspectives on different matters. When you make one person happy, inevitably, you will make another person mad and offended. To please everyone, you have to become a world class liar and manipulator. In the end, people will see right through you and you will not please anyone. Making everyone happy is an impossible, impracticable game. Everyone wants something and if you give everyone everything to make them happy, you will lose in the end. It may take a while, but eventually it will come back to haunt you. Stick with who you are. If someone is not happy with you, congratulations, that is life. Verbal attacks belong to your "attacker" because that is how they feel internally about themselves.

What have I noticed about people who try to please everyone?
How do I react when someone lied just to please me?
What happened to me when I tried to please everyone?

Those who know don't talk. Those who talk, don't know.
~ Lao Tzu ~

Listen, truly listen to the conversations that are happening around you during the day. It is great to have opinions, but to talk about them without knowing all the facts goes against integrity. Self-made multi-billionaire Charles Munger advises to not even form a belief about something until you are able to argue the other side better than they can argue it themselves. We see extremely biased opinions in the media every day. Some may even say that this statement is biased. Begin to form the belief of "you don't know what you don't know." The great philosopher Plato put it best: "Wise men speak because they have something to say; fools because they have to say something."

What conversations should I not be a part of any more?
What conversations am I knowledgable enough to indulge in?
What conversations do I want to be a part of?
What do I still need to learn?

If you must speak ill of another, do not speak it, write it in the sand near the waters edge.
~ Napoleon Hill ~

When you hear someone talking negatively about another person, do you wonder what they say about you behind your back? No documented good has ever came about by talking ill of someone else. It is not just talking out loud, your thoughts are included. Whether you say it, write it, or think it, your negative attitude towards a person or group affects you a lot more than it will ever affect them. The last time you spoke ill of someone else, how much did your life improve after? When we dwell on negative thoughts towards others, our subconscious translates it as thoughts about ourselves. Whether it is a conversation or a thought, focus on one good quality, characteristic, or talent that they have. Either way, you will be the only one affected in the end. The choice is yours!

How did my life improve after speaking ill of someone or something?
For something negative I said in the past, how can I speak positively about it in the future?
What does it mean to "write it in the sand near the waters edge?"
How can I apply that?

Not everything that can be counted counts, and not everything that counts can be counted.
- Albert Einstein -

Determine what matters most to you in your life. No one can tell you except for you. Most things that matter to people are not things that can be counted in terms of physical possessions with tally marks. There are some areas that can be tallied, such as a bank account. In the end, however, your bank account does not matter or count for true happiness. You cannot physically count the love you give or receive. One could have thousands of friends but be lonely with no one to talk to. Then there are people who have one friend, which is better than thousands of people who you just hang out with and use you. You cannot count honesty, loyalty, love, respect, determination, focus, ambition, integrity, ambition, focus, strength, etc.

In the end, what really matters most to me?
What counts to me which cannot be counted?
What can I physically count that matters to me?

Learn to work harder on yourself than you do on your job.
- Jim Rohn -

When one begins to work harder on themselves than anything else, it is done by doing a truthful exploration of your own life. When looking for everything in your life which needs an upgrade, be very focused, specific, and honest. Once you have a clear list of what can be developed further, begin by acquiring the knowledge and resources to correct the issue. A great place you can start is with books, audio programs, videos, seminars, trainings, workshops, etc. to enhance the specific areas you are developing. Begin to learn from others who have already achieved what you are working towards. After you have been working on yourself harder than your job, you will definitely increase your confidence, income, creativity, relationships, and more.

What do I need to improve within myself?
What are the first three improvements I will make?
What resources do I have or need for each one?

Pay attention to negative feedback, and solicit it, particularly from friends.
~ Elon Musk ~
Constructive criticism helps us grow but can be difficult to accept. Getting feedback from loving friends and family is a great place to start because you know they want nothing but the best for you. Some friends may be brutally honest and others may not for fear of hurting your feelings. Then there will be people who are just negative towards everything that you are doing. When you seek feedback from others, besides friends and family, be open to what they say because there is always some truth behind it. It may hurt at times to hear the things people tell you about something you just poured your heart and soul in to. Seeking evaluation from others is key because we all naturally begin to get tunnel vision with our projects and need help from many third party perspectives. You do not have to do everything everyone says, but it is another way for you to come up with improvements and new ideas.

What is something I should seek feedback for?
Who are ten people in my life I can ask for feedback?
What questions should I take with me to ask for specific feedback?

Teach thy tongue to say, "I do not know," and thou shalt progress.
~ Maimonides ~
It is better to say "I do not know" than to act like you do. The world is full of know-it-alls, we do not need another one. After saying "I do not know," you can add something along the lines of "but I do know where to find the answer" or "let me do some research and I will get back to you." People will have more respect for you if you do this than if you act like you know everything. No one can know everything. Experts do not even know everything that they are considered experts in, but they are constantly learning. It is great to know something, but it is even better to admit when you do not know. When you say you know, you are expected to act as follows. If you do not know and admit it, there is a lot less pressure on you. Stop lying to yourself and the world, life will be easier!

What happened when I acted like I knew something which I did not?
What do I not know which I would like to know more about?
What did I think and how did I feel when I met a know-it-all?

I am still learning.
~ Michelangelo ~
What a great example of someone practicing humility. Michelangelo was considered to be the greatest living artist in his lifetime. He was an Italian engineer, painter, sculptor, poet, and architect during the Renaissance era. Sculpting the famous

statue of David before his thirties and was the architect of St. Peter's Basilica in his seventies, he was constantly learning from himself and others. You are no different no matter how good or bad you are at what you do. Once you think you're at the top and can't get any better, that is when you stop progressing and possibly even digress in talent because of ego. Knowing that there is always room for growth is a key to success because now you will be constantly on alert to learn something new. Never stop learning!

What do I believe I am amazing at?
How can I learn more?
What can I do to constantly improve what I am amazing at?
What resources are available to me to learn more?

The man who has confidence in himself gains the confidence of others.
- Hasidic Proverb -
Are you more likely to follow someone who has confidence in themselves and what they are talking about, or someone who cannot look you in the eye? People with confidence are naturally attractive to others. People are attracted to those who are going somewhere, and want to be a part of it. True leaders have confidence in themselves. Having confidence helps you believe in yourself that you can accomplish your objective. Confidence shows that you know where you are going and how to get there. If you say something extremely outlandish with enough confidence, you can get people to believe you. When you get other people to trust you, it is because of the confidence you projected. No one will follow someone who does not believe in themselves or what they are doing; they follow confidence.

When have I followed someone with zero confidence in themselves?
How did I react when I noticed others were following me?
What do I have confidence in which will get others to have confidence in me?

Few things can help an individual more than to place responsibility on him, and to let him know that you trust him.
- Booker T. Washington -
Trust is essential. As we go through life we put our trust in other people. Once trust is broken, we close off our hearts to easily trust again. The more and more people who break your trust, the less likely it is to trust others again. When someone puts their trust in you, it is a great responsibility that you should be grateful to have. When you are assigned any responsibility from someone, they are trusting that you give it your best shot and get it done; especially when you say you will. Start thinking of promises as the biggest responsibility to have. A broken promise is broken trust. When someone trusts you, do not look at it lightly: you hold in your hands someone's faith in you. If you get in the habit of being untrustworthy, in the end, you will not even trust the things you say and promise to yourself.

How have I built trust in my relationships?

How have I lost trust in my relationships?
What happens when I put trust in other people?

Management is doing things right; leadership is doing the right things.
- Peter F. Drucker -
For those who are in management and leadership positions, being good at it is not easy. Some managers do not do things by the book and some leaders do not do the right things. Managers are paid to do things right so the rest of the company can function as a whole. By doing the right things, you gain respect of your subordinates and they will follow you anywhere. Great leaders give praise when due and accept full responsibility when things do not work out. Even when you are not in a leadership position, you can easily become the leader by doing the right things. Trust your instincts and conscience, forget about managing people, and start leading them.

When did I lead by example by simply doing the right things?
When was I a good manager by doing things right?
How could I have improved it by leading?
What is more important: doing things right or doing the right things? Why?

Innovation distinguishes between a leader and a follower.
- Steve Jobs -
Innovation is not only coming up with a new idea of doing things, but it is the act of actually doing it. Leaders imagine and implement new ideas, devices and methods to help change the world. Followers do what they are told and receive no recognition unless they are following a great leader. Everyone has the capacity of being a leader and a follower. Followers do not go after their dreams, they help the leaders achieve theirs. Leaders act on their ideas and take the initiative to make them happen. They create opportunities and have a vision of where they are going. They decide to make the choice to create the future they dream of. When someone has a vision of a "new world," it is human nature for people to follow them and bask in their success.

What was I a leader in, because of an innovative idea?
How am I innovative?
How can I become more innovative?
What do I want to be a leader in?
How can I make that happen?

True leadership must be for the benefit of the followers, not to enrich the leader.
- John C. Maxwell -
In 1970, Robert Greenleaf published an essay about servant leadership defining it as "a servant first," meaning, the people following you come first. A true leader takes the fall when things go sour and passes on the praise to others when things go

great. "A good leader inspires people to have confidence in the leader," said Eleanor Roosevelt. "A great leader inspires people to have confidence in themselves." The positions we have and the titles we are given do not make a leader; what is inside of you makes you a leader. Ideally, we all should develop the perception of importance of relationships and communication with others because without them, we could not achieve much. Everyday you are presented with the opportunity to be a servant leader solely to benefit others. Keep your mind open to this and you will begin benefiting others the way you have always wanted.

What opportunities did I take advantage of to be a servant leader?
How has a servant leader benefited me?
How can I be of benefit to others?

The function of leadership is to produce more leaders, not more followers.
~ Ralph Nader ~
The greatest leaders in the world mentor those who initially follow them and generate them into great leaders. By contrast, micro- managers force their followers to do what they are told, and look over their followers' shoulders until it is done their way. CEOs create empires by empowering their followers to become leaders who can explore and implement their creativity. Since the industrial revolution, employees have been treated as mere puppets, being told what to do, how to do it, and when it needs to get done. After, workers are micromanaged with a judging eye over their shoulder to make sure it is done properly. Fortunately, our society is finally beginning to make small changes to accept and nurture the voice of the people that are on the front lines of the organization. The best leaders the world has seen have been creating leaders, not followers. The best follower to have is a leader.

What makes me a leader?
What makes me a follower?
How can I produce more leaders in my life?

As we look ahead into the next century, leaders will be those who empower others.
~ Bill Gates ~
As we look back to previous centuries, the leaders were those who were born into royalty, or those who stood up against those who were royalty. Now that we enter this new age of the 21st Century, the new leaders are those who empower others. Merriam-Webster defines empower as, "to give power to (someone.)" The greatest of leaders give their control and power to those who are following them. Franklin Delano Roosevelt said "the buck stops here." Great leaders take the fall for mistakes and give credit when there is a success.

How can I empower someone?
What is it like to empower myself?

How have I done it in the past?
How do I envision myself being a great leader in the future?

You don't learn to walk by following rules. You learn by doing, and by falling over.
- Richard Branson -

When you watch a child learn to walk, there are zero rules for the child to follow. You could step in and dictate how you want it done, but in the end, the child will only learn by following their own rules and falling over repeatedly. Watching children is a great way to learn how to develop successful traits. Richard Branson is a self-made multi-billionaire who works extremely hard, but plays like a big child, even harder. He learned by doing, which is how Virgin Airlines was formed, and he learned how to play and have fun. Rules are in place to keep people in line, to keep them controlled and conformed. The best way to learn and thrive is not by doing what everyone else does, it is by doing what you know is right and learning as you go.

What have I learned by doing?
How has that benefited me and my future?
What have I learned by following the rules?
How has that benefited me and my future?
How do I learn best, by following the rules or by falling over? (Explain)

The next time you feel slightly uncomfortable with the pressure in your life, remember no pressure, no diamonds. Pressure is a part of success.
- Eric Thomas -

Diamonds are precious stones which are formed over millions of years from intense pressure deep within the earth. With millions of years of persistent effort and pressure, the earth produced arguably one of the most precious stones known to the human race. When you pursue what you are passionate about, you will inevitably come up against intense pressure from the opposition. This uncomfortable feeling is only temporary as long as you are resilient enough to keep persisting forward with your endeavors. If Bill Gates would have given up from the pressure, after saying his dream was to have a computer connected to the internet in every home, our world would not be even close to what it is today. The same applies for the Wright Brothers, Thomas Edison, Elon Musk, Mark Zuckerberg, Mark Cuban, etc. They all persevered in facing intense pressure and rose above it because of their resilience and tenacity.

What happened for me to choose to give in to the pressure and quit?
How has the pressure in my life made me a better person?
What will future resistance bring for me in my life?

Hardships often prepare ordinary people for an extraordinary destiny.
- C.S. Lewis -

Remember this quote from C.S. Lewis next time you are deep in a hardship and ask, why is this happening to me? You gain strength from hardships, failures, and defeat. Those who face their hardships head on are destined to live a more extraordinary life than those who allow others to deal with their problems. Everything in our life happens for a reason, even if the only reason is to help build you into a stronger person. What you are able to handle and deal with today, you may not have been able to years ago because you didn't have enough hardships to have the knowledge and resilience. Do not let other people fight your battles for you. You need to be the one to make the phone calls, have the face-to-face conversations, confront who you need to. It may be uncomfortable but handling it yourself will build you up and prepare you for your extraordinary destiny.

What hardships did I allow other people to handle for me?
How have I become a better person by dealing with my own hardships?
What am I prepared to handle in the future?

Defeat is not bitter unless you swallow it.
- Joe Clark -

When you start eating a food you do not like, chances are you spit it out. Think of defeat as food you cannot stand. You do not have to accept it. Spit it out into the garbage where it belongs and try again. In terms of food, you can try to cook or spice it a different way. Some people hate shrimp but will eat it at a few select restaurants and continue trying different styles. You could also order something completely different off the menu and not accept defeat that way. Once you accept defeat or failure, that is when you actually lose. You cannot beat someone who does not give up. When you persist through defeat and keep trying, you will succeed. Remember: success is always just one more try away.

What made me decide to accept defeat in the past?
What can I do to make up for that defeat?
How can I start over and do it differently with a new perspective?
What will I not accept defeat in anymore?

When everything seems to be going against you, remember that the airplane takes off against the wind, not with it.
- Henry Ford -

A plane takes off against the wind to create more lift under the wings. If it took off with the wind, the runways would be ten times longer. Airplanes also land against the wind for the same law of physics. The stronger the head wind, the shorter the take-off and landing distance on the ground. When everything seems to be going against you, it is actually there to help you. Diversity will build you up into a stronger person, develop more skills, and open up more opportunities that were never there. When you think everything is going wrong, you are wrong in so many ways. It may seem that way, but in reality, the Universe is positioning itself so that you can succeed. You need to persevere against the wind and lift above all the negativity!

How is everything going my way?
What is not going my way?
How can I look at it differently so it is?
How can I make everything go my way?

Don't let life discourage you; everyone who got where he is had to begin where he was.
~ Richard L. Evans ~

Everything that has come to be had to start from somewhere. No one got where they are instantly or magically. They worked for it. Life can be really hard sometimes. It is up to you to choose a life that limits you or choose for it to inspire you. Who cares about social status, race, age, gender, disability, etc.! What you choose is up to you. There is nothing stopping you from doing anything except you. No matter where you want to go or who you want to be, it is up to you to choose and be that person. It will not be easy and it will not happen overnight, maybe not even for 5 years or 30 years; do not let that thought discourage you. Don't give up. To go from the bottom to the top, it takes years of hard work and persistence. You can do it!

Describe in detail how great it will be to live my dream!
(Hint: Use the present tense!)
What is the worst thing life can do to try and stop me?
How will I overcome it?
Where am I right now and where do I want to be?

Little minds are tamed and subdued by misfortune; but great minds rise above it.
~ Washington Irving ~

Misfortune is something that happens to every person. Stuff happens that you cannot control. When bad things happen to people, they have the choice to lack intensity and strength, or choose to get excited and find the strength to rise above it. Small minds give up, lack self esteem, and allow life to control them. Great minds persevere and control their days and outcomes. When you come across some bad luck, get excited, because on the other side of despair is the mega-hit blockbuster of life. The only way to reach your ultimate sensation is to rise above and persevere through it.

What misfortunes subdued me in the past?
What misfortunes have I risen above? What did I do?
How can I emulate rising above misfortunes again in the future?

If the wind will not serve, take to the oars.
~ Latin Proverb ~

Sail boats use the wind to move across the water. Many times out on the water, you will need to reposition the sail to catch the wind to keep moving. If the wind does not help you go in the direction you would like to move, use the oars. Using oars or paddles to row a boat manually is hard work and takes a lot longer. Keep moving forward even when you are no longer receiving help from other people. Some people may say they will help you and help for a little and then disappear. That is not a reason to give up and wait for someone else to magically come along and help you out. Pull out your oars and keep making progress!

>What can I do to keep moving forward with no help?
>What can I do to get other people to help?
>How is using the "oars" so important to my goals?

Cause change and lead; accept change and survive; resist change and die.
~ Ray Noorda ~

This quote defines three separate types of people: Leaders, Survivors and Defiants. Leaders are the ones who control what changes and how it changes. Survivors accept what life gives them and do what they need to do to survive to the next day. Defiant people resist change by protesting in many different ways, from picketing to wearing clothes and doing their hair against the accepted norm. These people do not physically die but it makes them more secluded from the rest of the world who could help you. When you are just surviving, you become envious of the leaders and even the resistors. Leaders have a voice and express it, survivors hide their voice from the public and are complaining victims. Be a leader, not a follower.

>Which of the three types of people am I?
>What do I want to be?
>What do I want to be known as a leader for?
>What change in the world or community do I want to see?

Every adversity, every failure, every heartbreak, carries with it the seed of an equal or greater benefit.
~ Napoleon Hill ~

The laws of physics apply to your life as well as to the wider physical world. When you come up against adversity, failures, and heartbreaks, those situations carry with them an equal and opposite reaction which is far greater in benefit. For every door that closes, another door opens. This can be hard to accept at times because we are so focused on the negative that we do not allow ourselves to open up to see all the greater benefits which await. When encountering adversity, failures, and/or heartbreaks, you may have the tendency to feel provoked or to give up and quit. If you quit, then you probably will never even realize that there was a greater benefit if you kept moving forward. Create more opportunities in your life by knowing the best ones arise during the toughest of times.

>How has adversity, failure, and heartbreaks benefited me?
>What can I do to gain the equal or greater benefit of an opportunity I passed up?
>What was the greatest benefit I have received from adversity, failure, or heartbreak?

Be not be afraid of greatness. Some are born great, some achieve greatness, and some have greatness thrust upon 'em.
~ William Shakespeare ~

When William Shakespeare was alive, there were groups of people who were born into greatness. We still see this throughout the world in terms of Royal Families and Trust Fund Babies. But that is it. They have a predestined title which gives them the projection of greatness. Some achieve greatness by hard work, a lot of failures, perseverance and a positive attitude. Those that have it thrusted upon them did not fold under the pressure. Maybe that specific task was put upon others who failed and gave up only for that opportunity to be available to them, and they are the ones who achieved greatness. So can you! Those opportunities are everywhere. Open your eyes!

How did I react when a task I was unprepared for was assigned to me?
What can I do to achieve greatness? List 3 action steps I can take!
What is it about success and greatness that scares me?

Life is what we make it, always has been, always will be.
~ Grandma Moses ~

The reality which is in your mind is 100% false. What you think and how you perceive life situations are all in your head. During a police investigation there could be ten different witnesses with ten different stories of how they perceived the exact same event. Your life is what you make of it through your past experiences, your thinking and your perception on the world. This has been true since cavemen and will continue to be true millenniums past the Jetsons era. It is who we are as people. Our conscious mind has numerous filters that information goes through before it reaches our unconscious, where our memories are stored. Once it is in the unconscious, our unconscious runs our life by what we consciously allowed in. It determines our thoughts, actions and our perception of life around us. Life is what you make of it! You can change any time you want to by making that choice today! Make your life how you want it!

What life have I created thus far?
If I make no change, what will my life be like in the future?
What life do I want to create? How will I do that?

Realize deeply that the present moment is all you have. Make the NOW the primary focus of your life.
~ Eckhart Tolle ~

What happened in the past is over with, it is irrelevant. All that is left are the memories that either haunt us or inspire us. The future is all in our imagination. What one dreams of the future is drastically different than what your dreams of the future are. The past is as immediate as a second ago and the future is as close as one second from now. The only time we live life is in the now, the absolute immediate present. What you do in the now determines your future. If you keep putting off something for tomorrow, tomorrow will never ever come because you live in the today, the now.

>What have I learned from my past experiences?
>What do I want my future to be like? 1, 5, 10, 25+ years!
>What can I do now? What do I need to do?

Trust because you are willing to accept the risk, not because it's safe or certain.
- Anonymous -

It is never safe and never certain that people tell the truth. It has been proven the average person lies six times in the first 60 seconds of meeting someone. When you put your trust in someone, you are risking more than what you are trusting them with; you are risking your faith with them and your future chances of trusting the next person. Trust is an active process, not a passive one. If you trust a person to catch you when you fall, you have to be willing to let go, and actually allow yourself to fall, trusting that they will catch you. If you want the most perfect, beautiful, unblemished fruit, it needs to be picked when ripe, and you need to climb out onto the branch or climb a ladder to get it. There is no other way. Yes, you might fall. Yes, people might let you down. But if you hold back, if you are unwilling to take risks, you're going to wind up with bruised, damaged fruit. If you go through life not trusting anyone, you will end up not accomplishing much. You have to rely on other people and trust them to be able to do greater things. People lie, manipulate, steal, extort, etc. to get what they want. People are not trustworthy, yet you can trust a great deal of people with your life. When you accept the risk by putting your trust in someone, the greatest things in life can potentially happen.

>What good things came from me putting my trust in others?
>How do I react when others put their trust in me?
>What is the purpose of trusting other people?
>(Don't repeat what is written above)

If you're offered a seat on a rocket ship, don't ask what seat! Just get on.
- Sheryl Sandberg -

There are many different ways you can contemplate your next decision in life. Google's CEO, Eric Schmidt told Sheryl Sandberg, the Facebook COO, "When companies grow quickly, there are more things to do than there are people to do them. When companies grow more slowly or stop growing, there is less to do and too many people to be doing them. Politics and stagnation set in, and everyone falters." When looking for your next project or career move, find a place that is growing rapidly so you are always busy with work instead of criticism and boredom. If you are offered a position in a fast growing company, do not worry about the title, get on board. You will work your way up!

>What is my criteria when looking at a company, school, or organization?

> What is my required criteria in a company, school, or organization?
> How can I make sure that I find an opportunity with this criteria?

If someone offers you an amazing opportunity and you're not sure you can do it, say yes—then learn how to do it later.
- Richard Branson -

No one is born knowing how to lead others, make money, skydive, build rockets, etc. We say yes and seize opportunities to learn, starting from a place of not knowing. Parents present children with the opportunity to learn to ride a bike. Kids have no clue how to ride, but with training wheels, and from falling over and getting hurt, they learn. Next time an opportunity presents itself you're not sure you can do, say yes. Trust yourself that you will figure it out. People love helping people, do not be afraid to ask for help. The worst that can happen from saying yes is to learn that what you are doing is not what you truly love to do and it opens up other opportunities that are better for you; opportunities that never would have presented themselves if you did not say yes to that initial invite.

> What did I learn after I said yes to something I knew nothing about?
> How has my life changed from taking advantage of an opportunity?
> How can I create an opportunity for others?

Remember, you and you alone are responsible for maintaining your energy. Give up blaming, complaining and excuse making, and keep taking action in the direction of your goals – however mundane or lofty they may be.
- Jack Canfield -

If you want change in your life, you have to make it happen. Whether if it's your thoughts, weight, income, relationships, etc.; no progress will take place unless you use your energy productively to take the initiative and make it happen. If you are always waiting for someone else to make changes for you, you give up control of your life and put it in someone else's hands. This turns you into a blamer, complainer, and excuse maker because they will take the direction of your life to benefit themselves, not you. Life will always push you around if you wait for other people to do things for you. To them, their life and aspirations are ten times more important than yours. Start treating your life as top priority and take daily, consistent effort towards whatever goal you are striving for, big or small.

> How have I allowed others to negatively effect me and my life?
> How have I initiated my progress?
> What were my results?
> What results do I want to produce in the future?
> How can I make it happen?

I believe every human has a finite number of heartbeats. I don't intend to waste any of mine.
- Neil Armstrong -

Every second that ticks by, your heart will beat and you will spend energy no matter what you do. The richest people in the world have a finite amount of heartbeats just like the poorest person in the world. Age is relative because a ten year old may die tomorrow and a ninety year old may live another twenty years. Not one person on this planet will know when their time is up. We all have 24 hours in a day, 7 days a week, 365 days a year. It is a matter of how you choose to invest your most precious commodities, time and energy, which will determine what you create and leave behind. We all have the same amount of time and obey the same laws of nature, now it is a matter of investing your time appropriately. To optimize your time, creating a daily To-Do Checklist allows you to maintain focus and accomplish your most urgent priorities.

How often do I use To-Do Checklists?
How can I implement them more often?
What should I invest more time in?
What should I invest less time in?
Besides checklists, how will I maximize my time?

How wonderful it is that nobody need wait a single moment before starting to improve the world.
- Anne Frank -

The best time to do anything is now. You only live in the present moment, so stop waiting a single moment longer and start improving the world. It can be as simple as a smile to a stranger or mowing your neighbor's lawn without them asking. To improve the world does not mean to do something big and extravagant. You can do that if your heart desires, but to immediately start involves very small and simple actions that do not take up a lot of time or energy. Start treating people better than how you want to be treated. If you are surrounded by negative people, do not treat people the way you are treated, that will turn into a never ending, escalating cycle of negativity. Be the change you want to see in the world through your immediate actions, today.

What am I putting off which can improve the world?
What small actions can I immediately implement to improve the world?
What improvements would I like the world to experience?

I find that when you have a real interest in life and a curious life, that sleep is not the most important thing.
- Martha Stewart -

Even though sleep is more important than both food and water for health, you may neglect all three once you start pursuing your passion. People who are perceived as interesting arouse curiosity amongst others. Having a passion and living it daily brings people into your life who are curious about your accomplishments. Develop a real interest in life by doing what you love. Going through the actions of doing what your ambitious about and dreaming of the end result has great potential of keeping you from sleep. To help, get your 6-9 hours of sleep each night, make a to-do list for what you need to accomplish the night before. Do not forget to meditate 20 minutes a day at a minimum.

What in life strikes my interest?
What strikes my curiosity?
What do I want my life to be like in five years? Ten years?

What you are afraid of is never as bad as what you imagine. The fear you let build up in your mind is worse than the situation that actually exists.
~ Spencer Johnson ~
You will not get what you want out of life until you ask for it. You will not find anything unless you know what you are looking for. No door in life will open until you knock. Create opportunities in your life by asking the "dumb" questions, knowing what you want and showing up to open more doors of opportunity. Go out and take risks to live a fulfilled life! Once you overcome your self-imposed limitations within your mind which you created, that is when real progress takes place in the world around you.

What fears are holding me back?
What is something that I need to ask for?
What has stopped me in the past from asking this?
What opportunities am I hoping to be presented with?
How will I make them happen?

If you genuinely want something, don't wait for it - teach yourself to be impatient.
~ Gurbaksh Chahal ~
The only time you have is now. When you want something, now is the time to go after it. Patience is a virtue in retrospect, but it also has potential to destroy your progress. It is a virtue because when you ask someone to do something, by constantly bugging them, they will get irritated and possibly not do a good job. Strategic impatience is a virtue because you only have so much time in a day, in a lifetime. If you want something, go get it! You cannot always be waiting on someone to complete a project for you when their goals and dreams lie elsewhere. Your level of urgency will always be higher when it is your own project rather than someone else's. When you are waiting for someone to do what they said they would do, keep working on everything else and start preparing for when you do receive the finished results of what others are doing.

What am I most patient with?
What am I impatient with?
What do I need to do to improve?

Successful people do the things that unsuccessful people won't do.
- Jeff Olson -

Imagine you jumped into a time machine and traveled 1 year, 5 years, 10 years, 25 years, into the future and saw what you have accomplished. Take a look at your life in those future years which you control. How you currently think, act, and treat others is a good prediction of what your fate will be. You, and only you, have the power to determine where your life will go, what and who you will become. However, to do this, you must have determination and desire to be that person, to do things you are not currently doing. You will have to think differently, create new habits, and act in accordance with who you want to be. This is as easy as starting right now! By doing "the things that unsuccessful people won't do," you gain *The Slight Edge* over everyone else. If you think of a way which you can do something to operate at a level of excellence, do it! Unsuccessful people either never think of it, never take action, or give up after one failed attempt. Choose what the winners in life would do, take consistent action on all the "hard" tasks and never quit.

If I do not change at all, what will my life look like in the future?
If I start doing what unsuccessful won't do, what will my life look like in the future?
What "things" do successful people do?
What do I need to do?

Some people dream of success while others wake up and work hard at it.
- Napoleon Hill -

To have the intention of doing something is only the potential for doing it, it is not actually doing it. To dream and fantasize of the good life is the same as not living the good life. To make anything happen, action needs to be taken. The best time, the only time, to take action is always in your immediate present; never later today or tomorrow, only in the now. Napoleon Hill said "a goal is a dream with a deadline." You can dream of success for one hundred years and die with no results because you were not ambitious enough to actually make it happen. Once you start taking action every day, that is when you will no longer need to dream of success, you will be a success. Granted, once you become successful, the likelihood of you dreaming up your next adventure and taking action on it becomes more likely. Never stop progressing and always take ambitious action.

What do my dreams of success look, feel, and sound like?
What are my next three action steps?
What is a realistic deadline for completion with this particular dream?

If you want to make a permanent change, stop focusing on the size of your problems and start focusing on the size of you!
- T. Harv Eker -

You are bigger and stronger than you think you are. When you look at a problem, that is all it is; a problem. Every problem that you faced and will ever face, someone else has faced that same problem and came out on top. Stop looking at the problems you have as problems and start looking at them as opportunities to make something better. It is a great chance for you to grow, gain new skills, open up more opportunities, and it will build confidence and a sense of self-worth once you overcome any problem you face. The sun will rise tomorrow, time will continue to move on. Do not let one little problem stop you!

What problems am I currently facing which seem bigger than what they are?
What permanent change do I want to see in my life?
What opportunities are presented by the problems I am facing?

Certain things catch your eye, but pursue only those that capture the heart.
- Indian Proverb -
There are so many little details in everything that can catch your eye. Every second we have two million bits of information bombarding our five senses, we can only process 126 bits of that chuck. Within those 126 bits of information, there is a lot that can distract us from our path. Make the conscious decision to only focus on the bits of information that follows what your heart says. Your mind is what you think and your heart is what you feel. Following the heart is not just what feels good by doing it. If that were the case, there would be no fidelity in the world, no honor, no love — people would behave worse than animals. The heart is far more than physical feeling, it is the door of the soul, the window to the higher self, and the seat of conscience. The heart is what tells right from wrong, discerns what is good and what is not good. The heart is a complex brain, communication tool and sense organ that is the direct line of communication with Source/Soul/Higher Self/God. Your conscious mind can get in the way of your heart at times, follow your heart and good things will happen. Stop letting life distract you from what you are pursuing and/or what you know is right.

What are my biggest distractions?
How can I eliminate them?
What does my heart want me to follow?
How can I listen to my heart more on a daily basis?
What do I need to do?

If you want to test your memory, try to recall what you were worrying about one year ago today.
- E. Joseph Cossman -
This quote has nothing to do with memory and everything to do with meaningless thoughts. When you worry about something it wastes your energy, time, and brilliance. Worrying has never accomplished nor changed anything. If you think this is about memory, what did you accomplish one year ago today? You are more likely to come up with an answer, it may not be exact but it is approximately one year ago. What you do matters more than what you worry about. Stop worrying and start living the life you know you were meant to live. Nothing is stopping you!

What was I worrying about last year?
What did that accomplish?
What would I rather think about besides worrying?
How can I do that?
How often do I write in a journal?
If I do not have one, why not?

We must believe that we are gifted for something, and that this thing, at whatever cost, must be attained.
- Marie Curie -

All of us have a special gift or talent. Some have more than others, but everyone has at least one gift that can benefit that individual and the world once discovered and developed. If it is not clear to you what your gift is, think back to childhood. What were you natural interests and abilities? What were you naturally inclined to do that involved making, building, or creating something useful, helpful, positive, fun, healing, or beautiful? Ultimately your gift is something you have to recognize within yourself. You can ask others to help you narrow down your talents, if you're not sure what it is. Parents and others who know and love us since childhood are in the best place to see our talents and help nurture them within us. Sadly, not all parents do that, and the result is kids growing up with undiscovered, undeveloped gifts and a great sense of a lack in self-esteem. Once you know what gift you have that you can share with the world, treat it like a rare flower. Start eliminating everything that does not support, enhance, or nourish it. One thing you can eliminate for sure: watching television or surfing the internet for more than 30 minutes a day. (Unless your gift lies in the media industry!) Sacrifice such recreational activities and free up years of your life!

What are my talents?
What are my gifts that I can share with the world?
What am I willing to sacrifice to attain my full potential?

When you stop chasing the wrong things you give the right things a chance to catch you.
- Lolly Daskal -

Stop wasting time. We all have at most 168 hours in a week and less than 40,000 days (110 years) on this Earth. Our time and energy are most precious. Once spent, you will never be able to get it back! When you pursue things that do not matter, you will not produce valuable results, and the process will inevitably hurt you. The right things will always be in the back of your mind and never catch up. Slow life down, even come to a halt to figure out what the right things to do are. One great thing to do is to pursue your passion because living your passion will make you happy, inspire you everyday, and will benefit the greater good. You can help your community by smiling, easy as that. Practice meditation to help slow life down, figure out what is right and determine your next steps to create something wonderful.

What are the wrong things I am chasing?
What are the right things I should be chasing?
How can I start doing what is right versus what is wrong?

Start where you are. Use what you have. Do what you can.
~ Arthur Ashe ~

You cannot start at the top, middle or bottom. You start right where you are now—there is no other way around it. If you want to work out but do not have a gym membership, use what you have at home and do what you can. If you are broke and starting a new business, use your intelligence and creativity to do what you can. If you are struggling with physical limitations, focus all your energy on what you can do. There is no end to how many metaphors one can come up with for this quote. The only way you can be successful is to first start. Starting is the hardest thing for many people to do—until they actually do it! Then use all the resources available to you. If you do not know the right people, make it your business to know the right people. Everyday, do the best you can!

What resources are available to me to help me move forward?
How can I gather more resources which are currently not available to me?
What can I do which I have not tried before?

There's a difference between interest and commitment. When you're interested in doing something, you do it only when its convenient. When you're committed to something, you accept no excuses, only results.
~ Kenneth Blanchard ~

When you make a commitment or promise to do something, whether to yourself or someone else, your attitude will instantly be to work very hard so you can support it the best way you know how. There is a direct cause and effect relationship here. What you do or don't do (the cause) will produce certain outcomes (the effect). Same with reasons versus results. Someone who is committed will produce a harvest while someone who is simply interested will develop reasons as to why there is no harvest. Know what you are interested in and what you are committed to, there is a difference.

What am I interested in?
What am I committed to do?
What will I focus all my efforts on? How?

'Impossible' is a word to be found only in the dictionary of fools.
~ Napoleon Bonaparte ~

Nothing is impossible! The phone in your pocket has more computing power than the space shuttle which landed on the moon. People thought personal computers were impossible when they were the size of an entire warehouse. Stephen Hawking has ALS and is able to write books and function as a respected expert in physics and cosmology. Helen Keller was deaf and blind yet became an author, activist, and lecturer. Alan Eustace did a skydive jump from outer space and landed safely in a predetermined location. We are sending robots to mars and landing them precisely in craters from 140 million miles away. Impossible is a word for people who don't want to put any effort into anything. Losers use the word, impossible. If something sounds hard, it probably will be, but it is never impossible. When you truly believe that what you are thinking is possible, you will ignite your creativity and come up with all the reasons why it is more than possible.

What have I accomplished which I once thought was impossible for me?
What do I perceive to be impossible?
What are all the ways to make it possible?

What's money? A man is a success if he gets up in the morning and goes to bed at night and in between does what he wants to do.
- Bob Dylan -
Money does not mean a thing because it will never buy you happiness. In time, that happiness wears off and you need to buy the next best thing to be happy again. Forget about money! On average, you have 16 hours a day to do what you want to do. When you do what you want to do, you will be happy, and in turn, you will be successful. When you love what you do and you actually want to do it, you will put more effort into it and be willing to risk more to get what you want. Prioritize your life around what you want to do and you will be successful.

What do I do everyday that I want to do?
What can I do everyday that I want to do?
What do I need to sacrifice so I can do more of what I want to do?

Fortune sides with him who dares.
- Virgil -
Through the act of risk taking, you are partly putting your hands in "luck" to create a vast amount of money or possessions. Some may say they did not risk anything to gain their fortune because they did all the necessary research to make that educated decision. It is not based on luck either. If you go for the all-or-nothing, you are taking a very big risk to gain a fortune. Do extensive research to lower the risk and make an educated decision. Many believe there is no such thing in luck, only the will to take directed action.

What risk have I yet to take?
What risk am I willing to take?
What are the fortunes I want to acquire?

I've missed more than 9,000 shots in my career. I've lost almost 300 games. 26 times, I've been trusted to take the game winning shot and missed. I've failed over and over and over again in my life. And that is why I succeed.
- Michael Jordan -

Michael Jordan is arguably the best basketball player ever to step on the court. Yet his success was built on a mound of failure. Every time Jordan missed one of his nine thousand shots, he could have quit. Think about the pressure to take those 26 game winning shots only to miss, he could have quit. He failed 9,326 times; that is 9,326 more times than the average person. On average, people attempt something zero times. For those that do, 50% give up after their first failed attempt. They give up before they start. Success comes after thousands of failures. You will never succeed until you fail thousands of times.

What was my intention of giving up after failing just once?
For what purpose do I give up before trying once?
What do I want to succeed at which I gave up on? What is stopping me?

The biggest risk is not taking any risk. In a world that's changing really quickly, the only strategy that is guaranteed to fail is not taking risks.
~ Mark Zuckerberg ~

You can hope for the best, but prepare for the worst. The best way to lower your risk is through research and preparation. Investing in real estate has astronomical rewards but the risks are bankruptcy and losing everything you worked for. To lower the risk in terms of real estate investing, research the area, the building, the tenants, other properties, the laws, the construction, and what the local, state, and federal governments are planning to do in the future. The only way a billionaire is made is through incredible risk taking. Take risks after proper preparation!

What have I learned from my previous risks?
How can I apply it next time?
What are all the risky opportunities that I have at my disposal right now?
How can I prepare to lower that risk?
(Be specific, don't repeat what is written above)

People with clear, written goals, accomplish far more in a shorter period of time than people without them could ever imagine.
~ Brian Tracy ~

Goal setting is not difficult. If you have you ever used a global positioning system (GPS) to drive somewhere you have never been before, then you know how to set and achieve goals. You need three keys to arrive at your destination. First, you need to know where you are starting from. Second, you need to know where your destination is. Third, you do not need to know every turn and construction zone before you begin: your just need to begin and follow directions. On your car ride, as in life, you can always turn around or take scenic detours. This is your life. If you want to achieve your goals have a clear destination of where you are headed and trust your instincts on the journey towards them. Note that limiting your focus and attention to 1-3 goals or tasks at a time drastically increases your chances of success. Focus on one goal-related task at a time. Stanford University research proves that multi-tasking is harmful in the long run.

What is the number one thing I want to change in my life?
What three things need to happen to make that change possible?
What are my three clearly written goals in accordance to this one change?

Winning isn't everything, but wanting to win is.
- Vince Lombardi -

We all fail and we all will continue to fail everyday. Since we fail all the time, does that mean we do not win in the process? No! Each failure brings you closer to success. One thing that can keep you from ever winning is to never try! You need to give it your best shot. What matters to end up successful is your drive, your desire to win. You can accomplish anything and the first place to start is by accomplishing your inner self, overcome your internal barriers and blocks. You deserve to win! Now, find the desire to win! Keep in mind at all times that you will not win at everything, but you need to try. When you do not win, do it again and again and again and again and again and again…learn from each failure, make adjustments with each new try until you do win. You will never lose if you keep striving to win.

What do I want to succeed at?
What have I not even tried that has been in my thoughts?
What have I failed at that I want to succeed in?

The more you praise and celebrate your life, the more there is in life to celebrate.
- Oprah Winfrey -

Oprah Winfrey grew up in ghettos, moved around a lot, got into trouble, was sexually abused by trusted friends and yet she is the wealthiest woman in America and a great icon for everyone to look up too. "Be thankful for what you have," she says, "and you'll end up having more. If you concentrate on what you don't have, you will never, ever have enough." When you see all the good there is in your life, you will continuously find more and more to be grateful for. You will always find what you are looking for. Begin by looking for ways to praise yourself and celebrate your small successes. Concentrate on what you can do rather what you can't do. Robert Kiyosaki can invest better than 99% of the world, but he can't play basketball better than a bench warmer on the worst Division 1 college team. Guarantee: If you praise and celebrate your life for the next ninety days, you will be blown away by how much there is for you to celebrate.

What in my life can I praise and celebrate?
How will I celebrate my small successes every day?
What do I have to be grateful for?
How can I remind myself of this every day?

People rarely succeed unless they have fun in what they are doing.
- Dale Carnegie -

When you are miserable doing something, you are not going to put in as much effort nor be as creative compared to when you are having fun. Being miserable and bored versus being happy and having fun are all different states of mind. What is fun to one person can make the next person miserable and vice versa. Through your thoughts alone, you can have fun doing the most meaningless tasks. You can also have fun doing the most complicated task one can imagine. If you do not have fun doing what you do, reflect on that and figure out what would be fun for you!

What is fun to me?
How can that benefit the community?
How can I monetize it?

Just when the caterpillar thought the world was ending, he turned into a butterfly.
~ Proverb ~

Great things come in time, and failure can be success in disguise, success that brings about major transformation. The butterfly is a great example. After crawling around eating and growing for a couple of weeks, the caterpillar slows down. It appears that its life is coming to an end. It locks itself up in a cocoon like a dead mummy, stops moving, shows no sign of life and then behold — a few weeks later, out comes a beautiful butterfly, able to fly and go where it wants! J.K. Rowling was on welfare when she wrote Harry Potter. Stephen King was dirt poor living in a trailer home with his wife and children when he wrote his first stories. Do not worry about the conditions of your life, know that by sticking to your goals and vision, you can be transformed into something great. It takes work, it may take a lifetime, but the beauty you will leave behind is endless. Some people will give up before they reach their full potential and others will not even try. You can do anything you can imagine.

What powerful transformation am I searching for?
What makes me a caterpillar?
What makes me a butterfly?
What powerful positive transformations have I already gone through?

It's your place in the world; it's your life. Go on and do all you can with it, and make it the life you want to live.
~ Mae Jemison ~

You are the only one who lives your life. When someone tells you how to live your life, they are going to go off and live theirs the way they want and you are stuck living "their life." Everyone and their mom wants to push their opinions and values upon others because they think they know better than everyone else. No one knows what you have experienced, what you go through everyday, how you think, how you act, etc. Only you know who you are and what you want. This world, this life, is yours and yours alone. Do everything you can with what you have to turn it into the life that you want to live. If you are already there, think again. There is always more that you can do to improve. Keep improving, you will never be perfect but you should try to make your life perfect in your own eyes. The world is here for you to create your dreams! Use it!

What can I do with my life?
What is the perfect life I want to live?
What can I do to gain more control over my life?

Money is a number and numbers never end. If it takes money to be happy, your search for happiness will never end.
~ Bob Marley ~
The richest family in the world is the Rothschild's. If you thought Elon Musk, Mark Zuckerberg, and Sam Walton were rich, they are poor compared to this family. The "secret" estimated net worth of the Rothschild family is over $500 trillion. Metaphorically speaking, their search for happiness will never ever end. Mother Theresa lived in poverty with people who were shunned from the rest of society and lived an extraordinarily happy life. Money buys possessions, it is simply a form of energy exchange. Possessions do not create happiness, they are able to make life easier and cluttered. True happiness comes from your actions. If you have a bottomless bank account, soon enough the action of writing checks to nonprofits will not suffice. Happiness comes from living your passions and fulfilling your life purpose. It comes from surrounding yourself with people who love you despite your bank account. Yes, money can buy you a trophy spouse who is waiting on their entitled inheritance, but it won't buy you true love. Your actions are how you will find happiness.

What possession made me happy when I first bought it but no longer does?
What did I do which made me happy without spending a penny?
What actions make me happy?

I fear the day that technology will surpass our human interaction. The world will have a generation of idiots.
~ Albert Einstein ~
As technology increases, our human interactions with each other decreases. Our society went from playing outside to watching TV inside. We went from walking to our friend's house, to calling and talking, to texting and emailing, and now we use social media. Our emails now do not even have complete sentences or correctly spelled words. When a group of people get together, instead of socializing with each other, we are now on our phones or tablets doing whatever seems more important than interacting. We rely so much on technology that when we do not have it, we do not know what to do with ourselves. We take selfies instead of asking a stranger to take the picture for us. Instead of parenting or babysitting, we are now giving the child a tablet to raise themselves. As humans, we adapt to the times and trends which we have done very quickly in the past decade with all the advancement. To have a whole generation of idiots is not a stretch in today's technological world. Do

your part and help make sure Einstein is wrong. Use your brain, not your device!

How will I survive when my technology stops working?
What can I do to increase my human, face-to-face, interactions? (Not video chat)
How has technology decreased my communication skills? (It has, don't lie to yourself)

What are you grateful for right now? Gratitude can shift your energy, raise your vibration, and make all your next moments even better.
- Joe Vitale -

Dr. Stephen Covey, in his bestselling book, *The 7 Habits of Highly Effective People*, teaches how to live a principle-centered life. A very brief description of this is that you have numerous areas in life which they all beg for your attention. Instead of having your life get consumed with only one thing, be sure to make time for all the other important things which you are grateful to have: significant other, children, work/school, friends, family, career, and more. Life is full of fun surprises, do not just focus on one area of life, take time out of each day to be grateful for everything you have. What endures is gratitude; you will constantly find more to be thankful for, and in result, will project a high energy vibration into the world making your life even better. Create a schedule to ensure you keep your life well rounded and full of gratitude with different routines to maintain your high vibration.

What am I grateful for?
How will I remind myself to be grateful for what I have?
What routines will I implement to remain well rounded and grateful?

Don't go through life, grow through life.
- Eric Butterworth -

Do not let life pass you by. Slow it down and appreciate everything that life is offering you. It does not matter who you are, life gives us millions of chances to learn and grow. To "grow through life" means to gain knowledge, experiences, wisdom, information, etc. The most wonderful thing about life is you never know what will happen next! When something goes wrong, there is always a lesson to be learned. Figure out what you learned. When something goes perfectly according to plan, figure out what you learned from that too. The best way to grow is by debriefing. Debriefing is to review what happened upon completing a task or at the end of the day to gather useful information you may have overlooked during the process. A big skill builder with tremendous benefit is to verbally debrief your day in front of a mirror every night!

What experiences have I grown the most from?
What are the benefits to debriefing in my life?
Realistically, will I do it and when?
What situations do I notice myself just going through the motions? Why?

When you come to the end of your rope, tie a knot and hang on.
~ Franklin D. Roosevelt ~

Picture your life as a long rope. The rope symbolizes your strength, temperance, patience, willpower, anxiety, stress, etc. It is "the last straw". This is your make-or-break situation. When you come to the end of the rope, you either choose to give up and fail, or choose to hang on and be strong until you succeed. When you "tie a knot" in a rope, it a lot easier to hang on, it keeps you from getting rope burn, slipping, or falling. Tie that knot and persevere through all the negative situations life will throw your way.

What is my "knot" in which I hold on too?
What thoughts can I have to not come to "the end of my rope"?
Who can I rely on to help be my "knot"?

To be prepared for war is one of the most effective means of reserving peace.
~ George Washington ~

Let's first take a look at the Cold War even though this quote comes from the Revolutionary War. Russia and the United States prepared for a nuclear war. Since both sides have enough warheads to send each back to the ice age many times over, we had peace. When other countries proliferated, peace was imminent because of the threat of mass destruction. How can you apply this to your life? When you proceed with a project, prepare for "war." In other words, prepare for the worst to happen. Any time you go into something prepared to handle the worst, it is likely you will achieve what you set out to because you were more confident in handling all different situations. Likewise, when you have that confidence and preparedness, it is rare that someone will confront you and try to beat you! Be prepared for anything and you will be at peace!

When have I been more prepared than others and felt at peace during the process?
What process do I have to prepare for?
When I am at peace and not stressed or worried, what can I accomplish?

The best revenge is massive success.
~ Frank Sinatra ~

Anger hurts only the angry person. It is psychologically destructive to have thoughts of hate and revenge about someone. While you are dwelling on the past, you are sacrificing your future success for self-destruction. Thoughts are things. Your thoughts are who you become. Best way to get back at someone is to let go of the past and be the best that you can be. When you rise to the top and make something of your life without them in it, that sends a powerful message. However, do not go after success with revenge in mind and feelings of hate, that is destructive too. Think of your anger as a weight around your neck, or a ball-and-chain on your ankle. Letting it go is not about them, it is about you. Focus on you and become the best person you know you can be!

What is massive success to me?
How can I transfer my thoughts to a positive inward desire?
What can I do to build myself up?

Life is a shipwreck, but we must not forget to sing in the lifeboats.
~ Voltaire ~

When the Titanic started to sink, some of the people on board got into a lifeboat and were rescued. Some lived longer than the average person lives, they had long successful meaningful lives. A lifeboat can save your life if you use it when necessary. Life is full of disappointment and failures; find the good in it and be happy. When things go bad in life, and they will, we must find our own lifeboats to sing in and be happy that we survived the shipwreck of life. If everything always goes as planned, you are either perfect, delusional, or not setting the bar high enough. Failure is the best way to learn. When you fail, embrace it and be happy that you made it through and can go off and try it again. Love life!

What are my "lifeboats" I can sing in after a "shipwreck"?
What was the worst "shipwreck" I experienced?
What did I learn from it?
How bad was that experience?
Rate 1-10, ten being horrific.
Explain!

The words we use do not describe our reality...they create it.
~ Matthew James ~

Neuro-Linguistic Programming (NLP) is the language of the mind to successfully achieve concise results. Dr. Matthew James has been practicing and teaching NLP for 30+ years. Practicing what he preaches, Dr. Matt consistently performs at a level of excellence, always achieving concise results which he sets out to achieve. Whether it is the language you use in your speech with others, or your internal dialogue with yourself, those words have a profound impact on your future reality. If we are constantly describing our current reality as flawed and broken, we will always be creating a flawed and broken future reality. Words are powerful! Start talking about your problems as opportunities, focus on your strengths instead of weaknesses, find the positives in negative situations, and so on. When conversing with others, use positive language; your subconscious mind will thank you for it.

What negative words do I use most often?
What is a positive substitute for each one?
What problems am I currently facing?
How can they be viewed as opportunities?
Describe my "flawed and broken" reality with positive language!

Remember that happiness is a way of travel, not a destination.
- Roy Goodman -

Making it a goal to be happy in life is saying that you are not happy right now. Being happy is a state of mind, just like anger and depression. Your state of mind is a choice, it is up to you. If you allow others to control your happiness, know that you do have another choice. Research confidence building. No matter what you pursue in life, remember it is the journey getting there which brings happiness. Arriving at your end destination should not make you happy; however, accomplishing goals has the potential to make you intrinsically happy. When you do the things you love that you are passionate about, it will automatically make you happy. If what you are doing does not bring you joy and happiness, then stop doing it. You have a right to be happy. Live your life as a happy person in search of happiness.

> What activities make me happy? (List more than 10!)
> What ideas make me happy when I think about them?
> What situation brought me the greatest happiness? Why?

ABOUT
LUCAS J. ROBAK

After making wine and flying airplanes, Lucas discovered what he was born for. While laying on a hospital bed a team on neurologists handed him his life's purpose on a silver platter.

Being diagnosed with multiple sclerosis (MS) helped him finally realize that he's here to help people become aware of health and wellness.

Soon enough, Lucas was an organizer for *The Wellness Fair* to connect accredited wellness professionals with those who desire complete well-being.

Before all this happened, while reading a book to a friend's son, Lucas decided anyone can write a book. To prove this, a year later parents began reading his first book to their kids, *I AM – Children's Book for Positive Thinkers*.

This fun experiment found its way into Bob Proctor's legendary personal library and is being read to Jack Canfield's grandson.

Because people were asking, in one calendar year, Lucas published 75 people around the world for fun. Seeing what a book can do for someone, he now works with wellness professionals to get their book published so they can reach more people.

As a multi #1 international bestselling author and a contributor to numerous publications like *Addicted 2 Success*, *Good Men Project*, and *Thrive Global*, Lucas also has been interviewed on many podcasts and TV shows about his story and expertise.

Anything and everything is possible as long as you truly desire it. Remember this!

Be Different! Be You!

Lucas J. Robak

www.LucasRobak.com
Lucas@LucasRobak.com

OTHER BOOKS
BY LUCAS J. ROBAK

Master Your Life: Transformational Quotes Workbook Series

 Take a journey to find your lost passions and use them to fulfill your ultimate life purpose. Empower and enrich your life through extraordinary words of achievement and success. Use this workbook series as a guide to live your passions, define your optimal outcomes.

I AM: Children's Book for Positive Thinkers

 By the time our children reach seven years old, their perception about themselves is already set. Before we reach the age of eighteen, we'll have been told negative limiting beliefs over 17,000 times. Use this book to instill positive thinking in the minds of your whole family.

The One Minute Authorpreneur: Entrepreneur Publishing Series

 By using a book as a marketing tool, you can leverage it in many different ways to achieve your desires. Instantly separate yourself from the competition by positioning yourself as the subject matter expert. As an authorpreneur, selling books isn't important when compared to how the book sells you. #1minAuthor

www.LucasRobak.com/Products

www.ingramcontent.com/pod-product-compliance
Lightning Source LLC
Chambersburg PA
CBHW022014160426
43197CB00007B/426